winning bicycle racing

winning bicycle racing

Jack Simes
with Barbara George

Henry Regnery Company · Chicago

Library of Congress Cataloging in Publication Data

Simes, Jack.
  Winning bicycle racing.

  1. Bicycle racing. I. George, Barbara, joint
author. II. Title.
GV1049.S485   796.6   75-32994
ISBN 0-8092-8203-8
ISBN 0-8092-8201-1 pbk.

All photographs by Robert F. George/*Velo-news.*
Photos copyright ©1976, 1975 by Robert F. George.

Published by Henry Regnery Company
180 North Michigan Avenue, Chicago, Illinois 60601
Manufactured in the United States of America
Library of Congress Catalog Card Number: 75-32994
International Standard Book Number: 0-8092-8203-8 (cloth)
                              0-8092-8201-1 (paper)

Published simultaneously in Canada by
Beaverbooks
953 Dillingham Road
Pickering, Ontario L1W 1Z7
Canada

contents

winning
bicycle
racing

chapter one

equipment

WHAT IS A RACING BICYCLE?

A racing bicycle is a very high quality machine that is strictly functional. Years ago anything with narrow tires was called an English racer. Nowadays the public calls anything with ten speeds and dropped bars a racing bike. But neither of these is correct.

Just because a bicycle has ten speeds doesn't mean it's a racing bike. Just because it has dropped bars, it's not a racing bike. The important thing is that the weight must be within a certain range. A road racing bike weighs about 23 pounds or less.

Part of the reason it weighs less, of course, is that it has no extras on it, such as fenders and luggage carriers. But the primary reason is that the materials of the frame, wheels, and other components are themselves lightweight.

1

The racing bicycle must be responsive to the rider's demands and also strong enough to resist the stresses of sudden acceleration.

Lightness is not the ultimate criterion, however. You have to find a happy medium—a bike that's light but still strong enough to race on. For a good all-around machine I wouldn't recommend choosing something that's ultralight. The components are almost the same on a superlight bike and on one that's three pounds heavier, so you're spending a lot of money for that three-pound difference.

PARTS OF THE BICYCLE
(ROAD RACING)

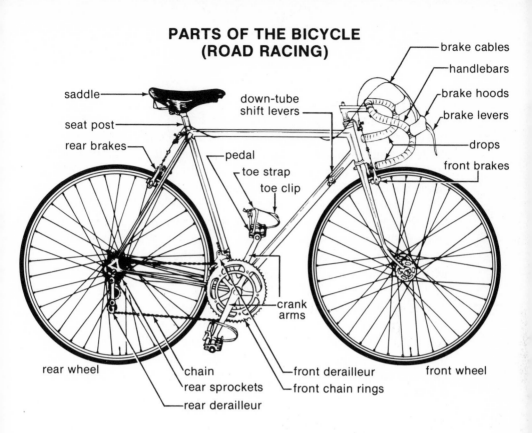

saddle

seat post

rear brakes

down-tube shift levers

pedal

toe strap

toe clip

brake cables

handlebars

brake hoods

brake levers

drops

front brakes

crank arms

rear wheel

chain

rear sprockets

rear derailleur

front derailleur

front chain rings

front wheel

PARTS OF THE FRAME

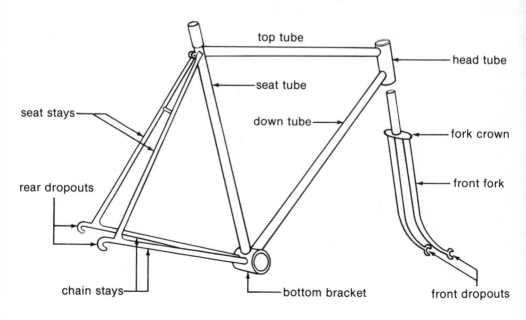

top tube

seat tube

down tube

head tube

fork crown

front fork

seat stays

rear dropouts

chain stays

bottom bracket

front dropouts

The Frame

A racing frame weighs 8½ pounds or less. There are many different brands to choose from and you can even get them custom-made to your own measurements. Concerning the brand of frame and the tubing it is made of, you should find out what other riders use and ask their advice.

For comfort and efficiency it is very important that the frame be the right size for the rider. When you're buying a bike, have someone hold it up while you sit in the saddle. With a few inches of seat post out, sitting in the middle of the saddle in bare feet, with the cranks parallel to the seat tube, your heel should just touch the pedal.

The saddle should never be flat down on the top tube. Always have at least a couple of inches of seat post out, because then you get the proper bend of your body over the handlebars. With no seat tube out, you'd be sitting right down on the frame and the bars would be way up in front of you. This would not be an aerodynamic or efficient riding position.

Although four inches is a good amount of seat tube to be showing, that is just a generality. A small stocky person or someone with long arms and short legs might ride with the seat much lower, since the smallest frame size is 19½ inches. It's the bend over the handlebars that's important.

The angles on a road frame are usually 73 or 74 degrees, measured where the head and seat tube meet the top tube. A very tall person might go as low as a 71-degree lay-back on the seat tube, while a sprinter may go as high as 75 degrees. Basketball star Bill Walton, for example, has a 71-degree seat tube.

The road rider wants to be close to the ground for stability. The bike with a lower center of gravity handles better, especially on corners and fast downhills, and feels lively. The sprinter, on the other hand, needs a more forward, higher-perched position so he can almost run on the pedals for utmost speed.

Wheels

A wheel consists of a hub laced to a rim by a certain number of

National team members Dale Stetina and John Howard need to
have complete confidence in their machines to take sharp corners
at top speed during a race.

spokes. In the beginning, don't go in for anything superlight.
Ride sew-up wheels with a name-brand rim, made good and
solid, with 36 spokes. A 40-spoke rear wheel is very good for
training because it will last a long time and won't go out of true.

The hub is the most important part of the wheel and you
should get a quality name if you can. Unless you have a crash
and break it, a good hub will last practically your whole career.
You might go through many rims, but a good hub can be saved
until doomsday.

There are basically two kinds of rims and tires. Clincher tires
are open and U-shaped, like an automobile tire. Clinchers are
heavier but cheaper and easier to repair. Sew-up tires are entirely
enclosed (sewn together) and are glued to the rim, whereas
clinchers have a bead on each side that fits against the rim.

5

Although it is physically possible to use clinchers for training and even racing, they really decrease your chances of doing well because they are so much heavier and less responsive. Certainly you can start training on clincher wheels, but plan on changing to sew-ups as soon as you can.

Tires come in all different weights; generally a 250- to 290-gram tire is good to start with. These can be ridden around the streets without too much worry about flats. And remember always to have a spare and a pump with you.

Nothing can be more discouraging than finding oneself ten miles from the nearest phone on a cold winter day with a punctured tire and no spare or pump. It happens to 95 percent of all cyclists at some time or another and one experience is usually a sufficient teacher.

On a typically Belgian cold damp dismal day in January soon after arriving in Antwerp to begin my professional career, I was training over a cobbled road through Flemish farmland when I punctured. Changing the tire, I continued on, only to suffer a second flat a few minutes later. What do I do now, I wondered?

Just at that moment I recognized Barry Hoban, a well-known English professional, coming towards me on his own training ride. "Hey, Hoban," I called. "I need a spare." But not understanding, and never having met me, he mumbled something in Flemish and continued on his way.

By now it had begun to snow, so with nothing left to do and with the flat tire thumping along, I began the wet ride back to Ghent. Some weeks later at the velodrome Hoban approached me and introduced himself. After explaining to him how we had already met two weeks ago on the road, we both had a good laugh over the incident, so familiar to so many cyclists.

But the lesson remains. You can avoid some very unpleasant situations by remembering the pump and spare—or spares, to be doubly safe.

Brakes

Brakes can be either center-pull or side-pull, as long as they're

Sprinting on the track, former World Champion Sheila Young reaches speeds of more than 30 miles per hour against her Russian opponent. Track bikes have no brakes or shifting mechanisms, and so are lighter and simpler than road bikes.

good quality alloy and they work freely and can be adjusted properly. Most racing cyclists prefer a side-pull when they have a choice, because it's lighter and has a more positive grip. The center-pull has an extra piece of cable across the top and many more parts to it than a side-pull, so it has a mushier feeling.

Brake shoes all seem to work pretty well. The softer ones may stop you a little better but they wear out quicker. Ideally the brake shoes should be toed in toward the front and touching the rim slightly. This position will keep them from squeaking and they will wear straight anyway, after a few stops.

The position of the brake levers on the handlebars is a personal thing. They shouldn't be down too far underneath where you can't rest your hands on them when you're on the top of the bars. And they shouldn't be too high, either, because you have to be able to grab them when you are down on the hooks. The exact placement depends on personal taste and the size of the rider's hands.

7

Stem and Handlebars

The stem and bars should be alloy and of good quality. The proper stem length depends on your position on the bike. Your hands should be able to rest comfortably on the top or bottom of the bars with elbows bent slightly, but not stretching way out. Your arms shouldn't be too close underneath you, however, because too much weight would rest on them and they would get tired.

The bars themselves shouldn't be too narrow, because that affects your breathing when riding. Although a narrow position is more streamlined, breathing is more important, so the wider the bars are, the better. Depending on the width of your shoulders, a bar that measures between 38 and 42 centimeters from center to center is usual. Forty centimeters is a good width.

The drop of the handlebars also depends on the rider's size. If you have really long arms you'll look for handlebars that have a little more drop.

Saddle

Saddles are made of leather or plastic and are padded or unpadded. Leather seems to be a nicer surface to sit on because you don't slide as much, but leather saddles take quite a bit of time to break in and they don't last as long. A nice combination is a firm plastic base with a sponge cushioning and a leather skin on top.

For short racing or track racing, use a saddle with no padding, but for longer racing the thin coating of sponge rubber underneath the entire saddle just below the leather or nylon is more comfortable.

If the saddle is too soft, you might get back trouble and pain in the lower spine from bouncing around. Of course, if it's too hard you'll get a sore rear end. Even the very best saddle still takes three weeks to break in.

If you lay a straightedge across the saddle, it should be parallel to the top tube. A slight tilt up or down is okay, but if it's tilted too far down you'll slide forward and waste energy pushing your-

With his massive build and enormous strength, kilometer champion Steve Woznick's start puts tremendous torsional stress on his bicycle.

self back. And if it's tilted too far up it could put quite a strain on your crotch.

A plumb line from the front of the saddle should fall about two or three inches behind the center of the bottom bracket or crank spindle.

Derailleur and Gears

The derailleur is the mechanism that shifts gears; there are

9

several good ones on the market. For racing, the derailleur should be light and should shift quickly and positively. The levers can be at the ends of the handlebars or mounted on the down tube. There are screws or wing nuts to adjust the tension so that it won't jump out of gear. The friction type of shifter is preferred for racing, although some people do use ratchet shifters.

With two chain rings on the front, five gears in the back is the most common combination. This has to do with the width of cluster that the hub will accommodate and still maintain strength in the rear wheel. Chain alignment is also a factor. The alignment in the front has to change only a little bit before the chain is rubbing on the front changer or jumping off the chain ring. Six-gear clusters are becoming more popular, but seven would probably make too much alignment change to be practical.

The cluster in the back is made up of the five or six sprockets or cogs on a freewheeling unit. Each sprocket is described by the number of teeth it has. A beginner might start out with a double-tooth jump in the back. A combination of 14-16-18-20-22 would be ideal, with a 42 and 52 on the front. This would make a good range without too many overlapping gears and with a convenient shifting pattern for riding. (See Appendix.)

Cranks and Pedals

Cranks and pedals should also be good quality alloy. A 170-millimeter crank is a good length to start with on the road, even if you are big. You don't want your feet to swing in too wide an arc, but you do need a bit of leverage for the hills.

Pedals are not terribly important, so even a steel pedal is okay. The ball of your foot should be situated somewhere over the axle and the pedal should be wide enough to accommodate the shoe cleat, but it doesn't necessarily have to be as wide as your foot.

Most pedals have slots on both sides for the strap to come through. Some people feel uncomfortable when the strap comes up from the guide hole and goes around the widest part of the foot because it rests on the bone. They run the strap through the inside guide hole and out the back of the pedal, but this doesn't give quite as much support as when it goes directly through.

It is useful to twist the strap between the two guide holes on the inside of the pedal. This will prevent the strap from sliding around and having to be readjusted every time you get on the bike.

Toe clips come in three lengths. Make sure to get the size that positions the ball of your foot over the center of the pedal.

CLOTHING

The most important pieces of cycling clothing are those that attach you to the bike or come in contact with the bike. The two things to get first are bicycling shoes with cleats and racing tights or shorts.

Shoes

A bike shoe has a stiff sole that doesn't flex. When you push down on the pedal the shoe doesn't bend around it; thus all the energy goes directly into turning the cranks.

Cycling shoes should fit more snugly than walking shoes. Try them on with a very thin nylon sock or dress sock. When laced up tightly, however, the two sides should not join over the tongue. The laces should be a little bit apart because the shoes will stretch after a while.

Cleats should be about a quarter of an inch deep and fastened to the shoe so that the ball of the foot will be positioned directly over the center of the pedal.

Tights

Tights and other cycling clothing should be made of wool, or at least half wool. Wool is durable and feels warm in the winter and cool in the summer. When wool gets wet it still keeps you warm because it breathes. Synthetic substances tend to get clammy; they hold moisture within the weave but they don't absorb it into the fiber the way wool does.

Professional rider and coach of numerous well-known amateurs, Jack Simes instructs cyclists in the techniques of team racing at the opening of the East Point Velodrome near Atlanta, Georgia.

Tights should be long enough to reach at least halfway between crotch and knee. They should have a good heavy chamois with no exposed stitching because seams chafe the rider.

I use Vaseline to keep the chamois soft and comfortable, but not all riders do this. After a ride the tights may be gummy from Vaseline and wet with perspiration. Scrape the Vaseline off with rubbing alcohol and throw the tights into the dryer. If they're made of good wool they won't shrink from this treatment and the extra Vaseline will go right into the chamois.

I don't wash my tights every time I wear them, but only every two or three times. When washing by hand, be careful not to dry the chamois too quickly or it will shrink. This bunches up the tights and, although the chamois will stretch again, the material won't, and there will be little uncomfortable lumps.

Jerseys, Long Tights, and Gloves

After shoes and tights, the next item to buy for racing is a jersey. This should be wool like the tights, or some kind of combination of wool and Orlon or helenca. Track jerseys can be silk, but these should be worn with a T-shirt underneath. If you can't get wool T-shirts, use cotton or something else that will absorb the sweat under the silk.

A very functional garment is full-length tights. These are worn over regular tights for warmth and should not have a chamois because that would put too much material next to the saddle. Leg warmers are good, too, but a lot of people find they have to pin them up and that can be inconvenient.

Gloves are optional. They keep calluses off your hands, they absorb the sweat, and they can serve as tire wipers. Padded gloves can be nice for long rides.

Hats and Helmets

Cycling caps are not just decoration, they are a really good cheap investment. The peak can shade your eyes from the sun or, turned around, can keep water from running down your neck when it's raining. The cap even keeps you warm, and wool ones are available for winter.

Helmets are required for racing and recent standards stipulate padded straps over the top of the head with no more than 45 centimeters' distance between them. There must be two straps around each ear and these can be padded also. Lightened versions of motorcycle helmets are also available.

HOW MUCH EQUIPMENT DO YOU NEED?

As with any hobby or sport that one gets involved in, you can eventually build up quite a big investment in cycling equipment. Initially, however, it doesn't take that much to get started.

For example, you can start training on a clincher-tired bike

U.S. track coach for the Pan American Games, Jack Simes helped bring the gold medal to the four-man pursuit team.

while waiting for your better bike to arrive. Sometimes it takes many months to get a good bike, but you still ride during that time. Or else you could buy a good second-hand frame from some other competitor and start accumulating the parts that you need.

The person who is really interested in doing well in racing is not very concerned about the prestige he gets from having a certain brand of bike or equipment. He just wants something that works efficiently.

A lot of people don't even care what their bike looks like, since it's bound to get scratched up in traveling and so forth. It's good for your morale to have a nice clean machine under you, but don't be obsessed with always having the latest and lightest available.

There is a lot of good equipment on the market, and it's not necessarily the highest priced. Races are won on all kinds of equipment and even the pros in Europe don't always have the most expensive stuff.

14

Author Jack Simes coached the two U.S. medal-winning sprinters at the Pan American Games.

If you took one frame and outfitted it with the highest quality components and another with the lowest quality, you'd definitely feel the difference in riding them. But if you changed only one part it wouldn't be that noticeable.

For example, you might not be able to tell the difference between a twenty-dollar shifter and a forty-dollar shifter. The more expensive one would probably be lighter but you wouldn't notice this in riding. However, if there are a few ounces extra on the gear shift and a few ounces on the brakes and a few ounces on the cranks and so forth, it all adds up.

Buy the best equipment you can afford at the time when you can afford it, in order to give yourself the best possible advantage. But remember that these things are really secondary to your training and racing.

chapter two

When you first get on a racing bike, spend at least six to eight weeks just riding alone and with other people before even thinking about a regular training program.

In fact, before riding with others you should just go out and get the feel of your bike. There are several important skills to learn that will make you a better riding companion and competitor. These are proper pedaling and position, smooth shifting, and relaxed and safe riding.

HOW TO PEDAL

When you begin riding there is really no necessity to go in a larger gear than about 70 inches, except downhill or with a strong tailwind. A gear of that range will teach you how to be supple, how

learning to ride

to pedal, and how to be relaxed on the bike. Don't make the mistake of forcing the pedals under a lot of pressure. I see many beginners and even supposedly top riders pushing gears that are too big for them.

In all bicycle racing, eventually you have to be able to get into the big gears and grind away. But you should know how to spin, too, because that's what really saves you and helps you last in the race. High-revolutions-per-minute, low-gear work makes you quick on the pedals and able to bridge short gaps. If there's an attack and a break is going, you can spin right up to it.

This is why it's important to learn to pedal. It's one of the most important skills in cycling and if you learn it you can do all kinds of racing. There have been well-known road riders who couldn't pedal. They only have one speed and they are good because they can keep it up and keep it up. But many times I'm sure they missed the quick breakaways by getting bogged down in big gears, and not having any snap in their legs.

As far as foot position is concerned, I think everyone develops his own pedaling style. You will pedal the way that comes naturally to you. You can try to concentrate on changing, but I don't think you ever really do.

In the beginning, keep the foot level. There have been great champions who pedaled with their toes pointed straight down and there are those who pedal with an ankling motion, pressing the pedal all the way around. Check out your foot position to see what it looks like. It should be fairly flat to start with and then later can go a little bit one way or the other.

Remember to pedal in a circle. If you take off the toe clips or loosen the straps you should feel that your feet are going to lift out of the pedals. Otherwise you're not pedaling in a circle, you're just chopping up and down. Feel your feet going around, not up and down.

The most efficient places in the pedal stroke are between about one o'clock and four o'clock but you should also consciously pull up a little bit when riding. Don't overdo it or it will make you tired, but don't neglect the upstroke either or you'll have a choppy style.

When taking a pleasure ride and relaxing I might do some coasting, but most of the time, even going downhill, I keep my legs going in a circle. This helps the knees stay loose and keeps them from getting too cold. I don't like to stop pedaling when I'm training.

It is hard to develop good pedal action just riding a road bike around, so you do have to consciously pedal all the time, even downhill. That's why some people ride fixed-gear bikes in the early season or train on rollers.

Although pedal action is the turn of speed on the pedals, it also involves sitting relaxed without moving the body all over the place and without sticking out the knees.

18

Brothers Wayne (left) and Dale Stetina have different builds and so show slightly different profiles in action. A streamlined position is important to cut down wind resistance, but the road rider must be comfortable, too.

The amount of body motion depends on what you are riding. When forcing the pace, or sprinting, or going into the wind or uphill there is going to be body movement. Even riding straight along the road there will be a little bobbing back and forth. Elbows will be bent slightly and shoulders may move a little bit, but don't feel that you are wrestling with the bike.

PROPER POSITION

When someone first gets on a racing bike he often says, "What are these handlebars doing way down here? I'm all bent over!" when actually he's sitting up straight.

It takes a while to develop a streamlined racing position. You have to get used to bending over. Go lower and lower until eventually you reach a point that's comfortable and still streamlined.

Don't go so low that you're kicking yourself in the chest. But work down to as streamlined a position as you can get without having back trouble and that's where you stop.

What you're looking for is a relaxed position without the bars

19

Track riders Roger Young and Sue Novara, both champion sprinters, can ride with their handlebars very low because their event lasts only a few minutes.

20

too far in or too far out, where you're just lying on the handlebars and stretching out slightly.

Once you've achieved something fairly comfortable you don't usually need to change position through the season. In a cold climate where you have to wear a lot of clothes in the early season, you might want to lower the bars a little when you get rid of all those layers. But other than that, there wouldn't be any big changes.

Riding by yourself or with others, you have to be really alert, always looking around you, riding defensively, and watching for traffic. For this a heads-up posture is needed.

Except when going into an extremely heavy headwind, you'd probably ride with your hands on the upper part of the handlebars, not down on the hooks. First of all, you can see more that way and watch for cars. It's also more relaxing. You're bent over a little bit, out of the wind, but not stooped over too much. It's just a nice comfortable position to ride.

There are several different hand positions on top. You can grasp the bars by the stem, near the center, in a kind of overhand grasp. Then there is the palms-up grasp on the outside of the bars. And sometimes you might slide your hands down onto the brake levers.

SHIFTING GEARS

A racing bicycle is not like a car, which starts in first gear and shifts to second, third, and so forth. On a bike you start in whatever is comfortable. On flat ground, for example, start in a medium-range gear.

Although it is theoretically possible to arrange a combination that would give you ten successive and different gears, most bikes aren't set up that way and racing bikes definitely aren't.

Think of the cluster in the rear as the transmission on a car. There are five speeds. Then when you shift the front it's like going into another range. It's like using a two-speed axle on a car.

Hand positions include the overhand grasp used by David Mayer-Oakes when he soloed to victory in the Junior National Championships.

The lead rider rests his hands on the brake
hoods while his teammate is on the hooks, or
drops.

There are the same five gears but they are all just a little higher or lower depending on whether the chain is on the larger or smaller front chain ring.

Two sets of five is the best way to think of the gears and of course they overlap. There is no first, second, third, fourth gear, and so on. Combinations are named according to how many teeth are on the front and the back. A 42 x 15 means there are 42 teeth on the front chain ring and 15 teeth on the rear cog.

Shifting is done by feel and by sound. It takes coordination between mind and body. There's no exact position for the levers. It doesn't click in and out of gear; it's a gradual motion. If you hear scraping or a funny noise, then you know it's not in gear properly. You can feel it go into the right gear with your legs, too, when it gets either harder or easier to pedal.

You should be able to shift without looking down. But if you have to, look and see how the derailleur cage lines up with the sprocket that you want to be in. If it's off to one side, then just move the lever until it's where it belongs. Or if the front one is scraping, then readjust it until it stops.

Often changing the rear cog changes the chain alignment in the front, too. The chain moves from one side of the cage to the other and can start scraping the cage. So sometimes when shifting the rear one, you have to readjust the front one, too.

A lot of people learn to shift both derailleurs at once with one hand. Do it with a twisting motion by putting your thumb on the left shifter and index finger on the right shifter. Or if you don't do them both at once you can still shift them right after each other by reversing your hand.

Sometimes a situation will arise where you want to go into another gear and into another range at the same time and it is very efficient to be able to do it all at once with one hand.

Both downtube controls and handlebar controls are good. It's really a personal preference. Sometimes on extremely bad roads or tight criteriums, handlebar controls are preferred. But just as many people like to use downtube controls because there is less cable slipping around.

24

National Prestige Champion Ron Skarin's specialty is the criterium, and for this event he favors handlebar shifters because they are easier to reach.

A fairly experienced cyclist can anticipate what gear to use under differing conditions. Notice how the wind is coming against you, or if you approach a hill think what gear to go into.

You should definitely think ahead on hills, because you're going to lose at least a length in shifting. Ease up on the pedals and then shift, because otherwise you can lose everything. The chain has to cross sprockets or lift off one sprocket and get onto another. If there is a lot of pressure on the derailleur, it's going

25

Think ahead on hills by shifting into the gear you will need, as the rider at left toward the rear is doing.

to skip, especially if you're leaning on it. You can miss the break-away by having the chain skip or fall off at the wrong moment.

Although it's easier to shift the front derailleur than the back one, here again you may have to ease up a little bit. Sometimes when putting a lot of pressure on the chain, you may try to shift down to the smaller sprocket in front and it won't even shift. The pressure is holding the chain right onto the large chain ring and the spring that is supposed to pull it over is not strong enough to counteract that.

Try not to use the extreme front and rear combinations unless you have to: the inside chain ring with the outside cog or the out-side chain ring with the inside cog. These combinations put a bit of a strain on the shifting mechanism and there is more friction. Particularly with a small sprocket on the front, like a 42, if you try to use it with the rear outside cog it may scrape on the big chain ring. With good chain alignment and an inside chain ring of 48, chances are it won't scrape.

Although I suggest the beginning rider stay in about a 70-inch gear, when going downhill there is no harm in going into a larger gear. As you get more advanced in your riding and start riding with others, experiment with the different gears to see what each one feels like. But try for a nice comfortable rhythm where your legs are turning around nicely and not getting heavy. That's the gearing to use in the beginning.

CORNERING

I think everybody who gets on a road with a lot of turns really likes to swoop in and out of them. You do it almost naturally and don't even think about it. There is a cooperation between your mind and body; you get your balance.

The line to take through a turn is much the same as in other sports such as auto racing, skiing, and so on. Make the widest arc possible, which means coming up to the turn on the outside, sweeping through as close to the inside corner as possible, and then continuing on to the outside again. Of course you have to be careful when riding on public roads.

27

When cornering, make a wide arc and keep the inside pedal up and the outside pedal down.

As soon as you can see the turn, set up your line. It's like a car driver on a track. Although he's going well over 100 mph, when he sees the turn approaching it's almost coming in slow motion and he can feel his body going right around it.

It's the same way in cycling. You adjust to the speed and the situation. Things start happening in your mind and you see exactly where to go and you do it.

As you come into the corner, change into the gear you will want to be in when coming out on the other side and brake a little bit if you have to. When coasting, the inside pedal is up and the outside one is down.

Sit back a little over the rear wheel, because this gives better balance when you turn and helps you to steer through. You can also let your inside knee hang out a little bit, to bring the center of gravity down. It's bad to get that knee caught on anything, of course, but it does help make you more stable and go faster.

Pedaling in and out of the turns is good to practice. Don't take chances by pedaling farther and farther into the turn until you scrape, to see how far over you can go. But do make an effort to judge pedal clearance, which determines when to stop and when to begin pedaling as you approach and come out of a turn.

CLIMBING

If a hill is not too steep, it will help develop strength in the legs to stay in the saddle as long as you can keep the gear turning. When it gets to be a real forcing effort, then get out of the saddle.

Climbing specialists are usually always out of the saddle and in small gears. The Spanish climbers, for example, don't push large gears up a hill. They're very relaxed and bobbing right out of the saddle, almost as if they were running on the pedals.

When climbing, the bike shouldn't move too much from side to side. As you push down on the pedals, your body moves from side to side a little bit and the bike does move slightly, corresponding with the effort of pulling on the bars with your arms.

But it's more important, when climbing, that instead of throwing your weight and bike from side to side, you throw it forward. You're hammering on the pedals and it's like lunging forward. Going from side to side is just lost motion.

There are many techniques of climbing but the important thing is to maintain your forward motion.

Years ago a European professional who had observed American riders told me that Americans don't seem to use their back muscles as much as Europeans. If you notice, most good bike riders have muscle in their lower backs, even the skinny ones. It looks almost like they have a little roll around their waist, but it's muscular and probably comes from pulling on the bars and a little bobbing from side to side.

HOW TO FALL

Crashes happen so fast that often there is no time to do anything about them. But through the years you learn that there are certain things to do to protect yourself when you crash. When it happens, the best thing to do is take your hands off the bars, grasp your head, and fold your arms around it. Even on the ground, again, cover up your head by folding your arms around it. Ribs and other places grow back together but your head can stand only so many injuries.

Some people seem to have an extra talent for being able to ride through an accident and stay on the bike. A lot of this is luck, but some of it is reflexes and some of it is bike handling. There was one fellow we called "The Magician," because no matter what happened he could stay upright. He could ride across an entire bike and not fall. People in front of him fell down and people in back of him fell down, but he could do it.

All riders do fall once in a while and I think it happens more when you are just beginning. Even in training sometimes you can't help it. If the front tire blows out there's not much you can do; usually you will go down. If someone else crashes in front of you, it's not your fault, but usually you crash, too.

Sometimes crashes are caused by taking foolish chances. In Belgium the riders are super bike handlers and they can jump up from the road over the curb and onto the sidewalk or bicycle path. I tried this once when I was in Belgium. The cycle path was muddy, so I was charging along on the cobbles. The curb wasn't too high, so I said, "Okay, I'm going right over the side." When I lifted my bike up to jump the curb, the front wheel made it all right but the back one grabbed a little and down I went, sliding about twenty feet through a mud puddle.

Riding cyclocross can make you a better bike handler. You learn to jump over things, to point your bike in the right direction, to handle all kinds of conditions, to ride close, and to be aware of things in your path. It's extremely good for teaching bike handling.

In this country I don't think you will encounter really bad road conditions in racing, especially in the beginning. But an experienced rider, particularly if he goes to Europe, might find dif-

Falls are inevitable, but try to protect your head.

ficult conditions once in a while. If a race is coming up over known bad roads, like on breadloaf cobbles where you slide right off the sides, then go over some similar road and see what it feels like.

Usually on bumpy roads you should push yourself back over the saddle to put a little more weight on the rear wheel. Especially on rough uphills the wheel can skip. A farther-back position seems to give more control. Ride relaxed with elbows bent to take up the shock of the road and keep pushing. Sometimes it seems to stabilize you a little more to use a bigger gear than you normally would.

The most common mistakes of beginners are riding too big a gear, being tense, and riding erratically or wobbling. The wobbling seems to come from chopping on the pedals instead of pedaling in a circle. Beginners also grip the bars too tightly. You have to grasp them firmly but be relaxed, too. From your upper body and shoulders right down to the wrists, you should be relaxed. If you stiffen your whole body and arms, you will ride erratically.

Being tense wastes energy and also makes a bad style of riding. With a smooth, relaxed pedal stroke, the bike will go fairly straight and will not have to travel as far because of any zigzagging from one side of the road to the other. This will make you a safer riding companion and competitor.

chapter three

After learning to ride straight, steady, and relaxed shifting gears smoothly, you are ready to go out with some other riders.

Although it's always nice to go out alone once in a while, I think there is more variety when you train with someone else. Especially when beginning, you will learn from the other, more experienced, riders.

It's nice to have someone to talk to on longer rides. And if you have any equipment trouble, it's good to have someone else along.

Although a national-caliber experienced cyclist can train by himself once he knows the ropes, even he would prefer to get together and train with another good rider. They push each other to do better and it helps them gauge their performance.

riding in groups

When I used to train with another American pro, John Vande-Velde, I could gauge my fitness easily by comparing myself to him. On my good days I'd be pushing him all the time and then on other days he'd be pushing me. Instead of soft pedaling here and there, I'd say, "I'm not going to let him get the better of me." This would make me go faster than usual and would help me in the end.

DRAFTING

When a rider is moving at 20 to 30 miles per hour, much of the resistance he feels comes from the air that he must push out of

"Sitting in," or riding close behind another rider, you do not en-counter as much wind resistance and so you save more energy than the lead man. Maintain about a six-inch distance and keep your eyes ahead.

the way. A moving bicycle with a human on it is not a very aero-dynamic shape.

The first big difference between riding alone and riding with someone else is that you can draft. You ride in the other man's slipstream and let him move the air instead of you. Doing this, you expend 15% to 20% less effort than he does. It's called "sit-ting in."

There is some benefit from the other rider's slipstream as far back as two or three bike lengths but, of course, the farther back you go the less it gets.

A good distance to stay behind another rider is six inches. A beginner finds it difficult to get accustomed to sitting so close. He's afraid the fellow in front is going to jam on his brakes. Or else he's just unsure of his own control of the bike.

But once used to it, you can get right up to within six inches and draft. I wouldn't recommend riding any closer than that, because of the danger of unforeseen possibilities. If there was a small change in tempo by the man in front, you could run into him. So six inches is a safe distance.

It's not a good idea always to look down at the wheel just ahead, because then you can't see what's coming. It's best to watch the small of the rider's back in front of you. You can tell from his body movements which way he's going to turn. Don't just stare at that one spot, though. Let your eyes flick from the rider in front of you, to his rear wheel, to what's ahead in the road, and so forth. But generally, focus in that range of the small of his back where you can easily see both the wheel underneath and what's ahead. After a while there will be no need to watch the wheel because you will automatically gauge the distance.

HOW TO AVOID ACCIDENTS

When riding in a pace line, it is up to the riders in front to warn of any dangers in the road. If there is a pothole, the lead riders should point to it. If they are riding along two by two, for example, and the pothole is coming between them they will separate a little bit and point to it as it comes up. Then the riders in second position will point, and the ones in third, and so on, and that way everyone will get around it.

On a rough road you might suddenly hear guys hitting holes in the back, and they will yell to the ones in front, "Hey, what's going on up there?" To help prevent crashes and save on equipment, you must warn them when you are in front and they will do the same for you.

Even a large field of riders can get safely around an obstacle if properly warned. You don't have to point right at the object, but just drop your hand in the general direction. After riding a bit you will automatically know what that signal means and go around the point.

I went out a few years ago with a group of new riders in another state. They all looked very good on their bikes but whenever they came to an obstacle they would call out "hole in the road" or "tracks" or "watch the cars." This really surprised me because where I ride nobody does that. If everyone just watches and stays alert and points, it's not really necessary to do any talking.

It is important to keep an even pace in the line but this is not always possible, and an experienced rider, instead of slowing down for an object in his way or jamming on the brakes, will be considerate and try to get around it and warn the ones in back. Sometimes there isn't time to do this, however, and someone may have to slow down all at once. This is why it's necessary to be at least six inches apart. With that distance there is still a bit of space to slide around the side of the rider in front of you if anything should happen.

Don't forget that if your front wheel overlaps someone else's rear wheel and the wheels should happen to touch, it's you who will probably go down, not him. Your steering will be affected and you will lose control.

THE TRAINING RIDE

On your first group ride, go along next to someone experienced and try to find out as much as you can. Get him to show you about sitting in and drafting and saving energy.

New people on their first ride tend to want to show their stuff and they will spurt up hills and so on. When the ride is going to go for 50 miles, you don't want to waste a lot of energy doing that right off the bat. Just ride along and see how you feel, listen to what the others tell you, and learn mainly about sitting in and riding smoothly and safely.

Training is not a thing where you're killing yourself every day. You have to be able to do it day after day, so you have to be fresh. Don't go in too big a gear because flogging a big gear on a long ride can make you tired the following day. Stay in a fairly small gear so you will still be able to get out and train the next day.

Tempo riding is a method that is just coming into its own in this country and is proving to be very effective. It is pedaling rapidly in a small gear and it works on your cardiovascular fitness.

Depending on what you have been doing for racing, you may not want to start the first miles of the ride going fast. With recent real hard racing or stage racing, it may be better to take it easy for a few days, starting your ride slowly and working into it gradually.

If you have been doing tempo riding every day, when you first get on your bike there may be a funny stiff feeling in your legs. They may hurt and feel like balloons. So when I first get on the bike I go hard for awhile, which gets rid of that feeling. If I push a little bit and it doesn't go away, then I take it real easy for the rest of the day.

Once you join your riding companions and are warmed up using whatever method you choose, take turns riding at the front so that everyone will get a good workout periodically and rest by drafting.

The length of time each rider stays at the front depends on what event he is training for. An all-around rider wants to stay up there until he gets fairly tired, riding ten or fifteen minutes quite fast. On a long ride, he may even stay up in front for half an hour occasionally.

Usually, however, the lead changes every five or ten minutes. That way everybody gets up there and does his work. Especially in a line of three or more people, you don't want to hold the others back too much, so five or ten minutes is about right.

Try to maintain an even pace at the front. On the grades you can really step into it a little bit. Both up and down the hills, try to keep the same tempo going.

You don't need to ride a lower position while at the front, but you may be a little more tense from putting in more effort.

Don't ride at the front until you go sour. Ride until you feel tired but will still recuperate. If you feel like you are slowing down it's time to get out of there. And if you feel like you'll leave your breakfast on the road, you've gone too far.

On a training ride the lead should change every five or ten minutes. The front man moves to the side and eases up a little, while the next man pulls through.

There is no special trick about getting on the back of the line after you pull off. On a training ride the other riders will come through at an even pace but not as fast as they would in a race.

Pull off into the wind and stay fairly close to the string coming through. Stay on the pedals and don't coast or else you will have to accelerate to get back on again. Keep watching and, as the rear comes by, just fade right onto it.

The pace of the ride will pick up as the season progresses. This is especially true in a cold climate where riders use long-sleeved jerseys, heavy sweaters, and long tights in the early season. Anything that grabs the wind will slow you down, of course, so taking these things off will help your speed. Also, the air is getting warmer and lighter and you are getting fitter. The revolutions per minute may not change that much but you will be riding bigger gears and will go faster.

RIDING FORMATIONS

There are several different formations to use in a group ride, depending on how many riders there are and how hard a workout they want.

I think three or four is the most efficient number of riders to train with, depending on who they are, of course. Groups larger than that seem to bog down a bit.

One thing that slows down a training ride is flat tires because if somebody has a flat and you decide to wait for him, it's very time-consuming. With half a dozen riders there is more chance of somebody stopping for some reason.

Three or four riders can go along nicely with just the right amount of time at the front and the right amount of time sitting in. You really do need the work at the front to get fit and if there are eight people, for example, you are sitting in much more than riding at the front.

In the early part of the season when there isn't too much important racing, you should slow down and wait when other newer riders can't keep up and try to help them. But as the season progresses, you have to be conscious of your own training and can't really be waiting all the time. It has to be made clear from the beginning that you will continue at your own pace and most riders do understand that.

Depending on the rules of the road in your state, two riders training together will usually ride abreast. This is a good chance to get used to riding close and being relaxed.

Bumping shoulders or elbows with a new rider is apt to alarm him. He may wiggle a little bit on his bike or even shoot across the road trying to get out of the way. But with experienced riders this has no effect. It's just a matter of confidence and of relaxing. When accustomed to riding with other people, you can just ride along and lean on someone and talk to him. Riding close together will get you used to the experience of being in a dense field.

It's also good to have someone next to you doing a little half-

41

wheeling. If he stays just a few inches ahead, you'll feel like you're chasing him and this will make you go faster. Of course it can be very annoying to ride with someone who is half-wheeling all the time, especially on a social ride.

Some of the hardest training is with three riders, when two are at the front and one is in back resting, because each man does a double pull. As one swings off, the man at the back comes to the front, while the other guy still has to stay up there and ride against the fresh man. Then he pulls off and they rotate in that way.

Though the echelon formation is common in racing, it is hard to use an echelon in training because it takes up too much of the road.

An echelon is a staggered line of riders, each one slightly to the leeward side of the rider ahead so as to get the most protection from the wind.

The shape of the echelon depends on where the wind is coming from. If it's from directly ahead there will just be a string of riders. If the wind is coming from an angle off to the left side, you stay to the right side of the rider in front of you, to get as much draft as possible. If the wind is coming directly across the road, riders might almost overlap up to each other's bottom bracket, although this is dangerous when you are just beginning.

The echelon is a big rotating circle because, as the front rider eases to drop to the rear, the second man comes through and will pull in front of him and ease off, and the third will come through and pull in front of the new leader, and so on.

As the echelon starts passing, when the second man is by you and there is room so you won't run into him, you can drop in back of him. As the third man passes the second man you drop in back of him, and ride the echelon right back across.

If the wind is coming from an angle, obviously even three men in an echelon can take up the whole road, so the echelon is hardly ever used in training or group rides.

The riding formation used most in Europe and that I use in my group training rides is the two-by-two method.

42

An echelon is a staggered line of riders that forms when there is a side wind. Each one tries to get the most protection from the one ahead.

When the two men at the front have finished their turn, each pulls off on his own side and the rest of the pace line, in double file, comes up through the middle. The man on the right moves slightly to the right and eases off, and the man on the left swings out a little bit to the left, and the whole line comes right through.

RIDING IN A FIELD

Riding in a large field of riders, as in a mass start race, multiplies all the problems of riding in small groups. The pack is very close together, not one by one, or two by two, but like a swarm of bees.

Don't make any sudden unexpected moves in the field and watch out for erratic moves by others. If the rider in front of you is not aware that you are passing or coming up on him, it is quite all right to take one hand off the bars and touch him on the hip.

Try to ride smoothly while in a large field. Concentrate on safety and don't make any sudden moves.

An experienced rider would be grateful for that signal and that you didn't cause a crash or run into anybody.

If, for example, you are moving up where there is room on the curb side and suddenly somebody in front moves in that direction, you could say "on the left." But it is always much safer to put your hand out and touch him, because then you can hold yourself away from him, too.

When first starting, the farther toward the front you can be, the better, because it lessens the chances of a crash. Having fifty people in front of you wiggling around is a lot worse than having only ten. A good position to ride is somewhere in the first fifteen, so you can still see where you're going.

Of course you can't always be in the front and will find yourself filtering back. When you do get back in the field, start thinking about getting out of there. In a really tightly packed field that's not moving too fast, you are usually stuck in the middle for quite a while and can't instantly get out. But there are always holes opening up here and there and, moving from one spot to another, it doesn't take long to get in a good position again.

When you see an opening where you can move to the side, that is a better place to be, too, as long as no one is forcing you into the curb.

Going around turns, also, there are little gaps left, which you can fill in without pushing or cutting anybody off or moving erratically. You can slip through the field as it moves and sways around bends.

Even if the field is going in a straight line, people are riding at different speeds and so there are always little holes opening up that you can slip into, one or two at a time, and change position that way.

The field is constantly rotating and circulating. Riders are trying to get to the front and, as they get there, it puts the others farther back and so on. Some riders stay in the front for the whole race and others stay at the back, but generally it's circulating slowly.

Riding in the field, you can't always take exactly the line you want on corners. If on the inside, you may have to slow down to make a sharper turn, and the riders on the outside will be going faster than you are. Coming out of the turn, they will be ahead and you will have to accelerate to catch up. If you get caught on the inside and are going too fast, centrifugal force will push you into the riders on the outside. If you overlap a wheel you're finished.

The best way to take corners in a big field is just to follow the rider in front and not to overlap. It's better to be on the outside than on the inside, but the outside has disadvantages, too, because the inside riders can knock you down. So, in a turn, especially when the group is small, ride one behind the other.

Safety is the most important consideration in the field, but generally just use what you've learned in riding with one or two people. You should be able to ride next to others and touch them without getting shaken up. Just relax on your bike, always look around, keep a good distance from the rider in front of you so you won't be bumping his wheel, and you'll learn.

45

chapter four

There are many different ways to win a race, depending on what kind of race it is and what type of rider you are.

If you are very strong but slow, don't wait for the sprint. Attack early and force the pace at every opportunity. Hopefully, this will weaken the field, which will dwindle in size.

If your main forte is sprinting, of course, you don't even want to attack. As the end of the race nears, stay close to the front to make sure nobody sneaks away. If anything goes, jump right on it and go with it. But don't attack by yourself at all, just sit in and wait for the end.

POSITION IN THE FIELD

Don't worry about which riders to stay near in the field. Ride po-

tactics: how to win a race

sition, not the rider. In other words, know the course, and when the finish is coming up, don't be concerned too much about the others.

Funny combinations of riders can succeed in breaking away. Three or four unexpected people can go, and if the right guys are out there working and the right circumstances happen back in the field, they're on their way. It's important to stay near the front, so you can be ready if this happens.

It is a good idea before the race to sit down and look at a program to see who has what number. Keep these numbers in mind and when a few of them go away, then you know it's time to go, too. Maybe the break is not going to succeed, but you have to go with them just to make sure.

It's good to stay near the front of the field in case a break develops.

It's also important to stay near the front of the field if there are any primes. Primes are prizes within the race and may be awarded to the leader at a certain distance or on a certain lap, the winner of a sprint at a certain place on the course, the first rider to lap the field, or any other test that the promoter can think of.

It's always good to get a prime, especially if it's early in the race, because it helps to test your legs. Also, in case something happens later on in the race and you don't get anything in the eventual finish, you still have something to show for your efforts that day.

It can be difficult to stay near the front and probably that's

48

why the stronger riders eventually break away. In Europe, for example, everyone is trying to get to the front and those in the front are trying to attack off the front. The weaker ones hang in the back until eventually they just fall behind.

There's no special trick to staying in front: it's mainly what you have in your legs. You must be aggressive; there's no room for wheel-suckers up there. You have to really work to stay in front because riders are always coming from the back who have the same idea. That's what makes the field circulate.

Eventually the strongest riders will go off the front because all you need when it's really moving is one or two weak links in the middle. For instance, if an echelon or a string develops and a couple of people can't keep up the pace, they leave gaps and then the break is gone.

HOW TO BREAK AWAY FROM THE FIELD

There are many different methods of breaking away from the field. You can take a flyer by laying back a little, leaving a bit of a gap, and then making a tremendous rush to bridge it.

You can also ride right off the front, which is done in many races in Europe. Ride very hard tempo and don't leave room for people to sit on. If there's a side wind coming, say, from the left, get on the right side of the road where there's no way for anybody to echelon, and start pouring it on. A string of riders will form behind you and if somebody blows up, maybe four or five riders back, then there are just three riders away.

Another way of doing it is by hammering away, mile after mile, until the riders in the field just say, "Aw, I'm not chasing him any more again. I'll just rest a minute and get him later." And then off you go.

Teammates can help the breakaway attempt by blocking any chasers in the field. One way is to get in front and actually spread across the road.

If a lone rider wants to help someone else's chances he can ride a little bit of tempo and as the chasers start to pass, he drifts in their direction and makes them go around the long way. Or he can move closer to the curb so they'll have to back out and go around the other side.

Another way of blocking is to sit in and mess up the pace line. As soon as someone starts to chase, the blockers join in and get on the attackers' wheels. When a chaser swings off, hoping the next rider will come by, the blocker just pedals through and slows the pace down immediately. If someone else attacks, another teammate can jump on and slow it down again when his turn comes at the front. This messes up everything and, by the time the chasers get organized to attack again, there's a good chance that the breakaway is gone.

The teammates of these breakaway riders can hold back the field by blocking at the front.

Hills are an excellent place to break away if you are a strong climber.

WHERE TO BREAK AWAY

There are no set rules about when and where to break away. The slow but strong rider has to attack right from the beginning, whether it's a 50-mile race or a 150-mile race. A rider who's strong but fast, too, might wait until there's three miles to go and then, bang, he's off. He can ride such a tremendous tempo from that time until the end that it's going to be pretty tough to get him.

If you're known to be a hill climber, then you want to make your attacks on the hills, forcing the pace and hoping to get far enough away so they won't catch you on the descents. Riders even get away going downhill if they are very daring or very streamlined or have a very big gear.

Corners are a good place to get away, especially if you have a bike with a high bottom bracket. If you attack just before a turn then you're moving faster than your opponents. Even if you have to coast you're still moving faster and they can't pick it up in the turn because they can't pedal then. You hit it earlier than they do and get another two or three lengths. When the others are setting up for a turn, it is sometimes possible to slip through on the inside or outside and get three or four lengths before they can take up the chase.

If you are going to attack immediately after the turn or pedal all the way through where before everyone was coasting, you might not shift down for the corner. You might even put it in a bigger gear, for attacking, push it through the turn, and then get right on it. The other riders will have to jump after you and change gears later.

Another place to make the big break in a race is just after the prime. If the right riders sprint for the prime, stay close to them, and after they sprint and start slowing down, then you go. Even if a few riders go with you, after a big prime is a good time to attack because those who have made their effort might be tired.

RIDING IN THE BREAKAWAY

Between six and nine riders is a good number to have in a breakaway. With a small break of only three riders, each one has to pull 150 to 300 yards, taking his turn at the front and then swinging off. But a larger number can form a fast circular pace line.

As each rider gets into the front position, the next one passes him and rides over in front of him. Just as he does that, the next one comes by. It's like a big circle going around. When you get to the front, ride over in front of the one who has just been in front of you and then ease pedaling. It's almost as if you never hit the front. You come up there often but you don't stay long. All you have to do is ride by one man and then you're done.

Chances are if it's a good break there won't be too many weak riders in it and everyone will do his share. But if you have somebody who's not working, who's just sitting on the back, there are ways of getting rid of him.

53

Between six and nine riders is a good number to have in a break-away group because it makes an efficient pace line.

If there is one rider hanging on the back, as you come to the back after your pull, swing in front of him and let the group go. This will force him to come around you in order to catch them. If he still just sits there, you can attack him by jumping up and joining the group yourself quickly, hopefully leaving him behind or making him chase, too.

Another way to get rid of a sleigh rider is to get together with the other riders, make an echelon, and don't leave room for him. For instance, if there's a seven-man break, start the echelon half way over to the side of the road so that there's only room for six. That will leave him hanging on the back and he'll probably go off, if the pace is hard enough.

A third way is to have your teammates attack one by one, making sure not to chase one another. When the sleigh rider takes up chase, attack him again as soon as he's finished his effort, whether it be because he's caught the breakaway rider, has swung off for someone else to take pace, or is just plain slowing down from fatigue. Repeat this process a few times and he'll come undone for sure.

All these tactics depend on who the other rider is and on his character. If he's a tough individual you may not be able to get rid of him. He may be hanging on by his teeth and not feeling too happy either, but there's not much you can do about it.

You may also want to tire out some one particular rider. If you are ahead of him when doing your pull, start accelerating just as you're getting ready to swing off. This leaves him with a faster pace to maintain.

Or else you can hammer through on him. If you are in back of him as he swings off, then come through fast so that he has to make an extra effort to get back on. After a period of time that can really weaken somebody.

You can also demoralize a rider by yelling at him and telling him he's not doing his share. This won't work with somebody experienced, but if he's not too hip to what's going on he'll start doing a little extra.

It helps to know your opponent, both his weaknesses and his personality. If you know what agitates him, do that constantly. Some riders will blow their cool if you agitate them verbally or hook them around a little bit.

If you can beat someone at his own game it really shocks him. Perhaps your opponent is a good road rider who likes to pull and is known for his superior strength in this department. Get right behind him in the echelon and, as his turn comes up to pull, pass him immediately and don't even let him stay out there. You can beat him at his own game by not even letting him do it in the first place.

Many riders are not aware of the possibilities of psychological warfare. They don't even make use of such simple and obvious tactics as attacking when their opponent is not looking, when he's tired, or when he's caught behind someone else.

Even being a good actor can help you win a race. Once I was in a final breakaway with several other riders who were fitter than I was at the time. They were sprinting for the primes but I was saving everything. I was so tired that if they had made an attack I would have been finished. But they didn't realize that, because I didn't show it. I tried to look fresh, like it wasn't bothering me, when all the time I was aching inside. By hiding my condition and pretending to feel fine, I managed to make it to the end and beat them in the sprint.

The way to prevent the other riders from knowing when you are suffering is to keep your mouth closed and look alert. Inside, your guts may be falling out, but you look fresh as a daisy.

Sometimes, on the other hand, it's beneficial to appear tired. You can pull a lot on your bars and wrestle with your bike. Breathe hard and try to look red in the face. People will notice this. They are watching and their eyes are flicking around all the time.

If another rider really knows what he's doing, he can make it hard for you to tell how he's feeling. But if you're dealing with someone who's not quite in shape, for example, you can listen to his breathing. Compare it to your own breathing and see if he's taking shorter or faster breaths. Look at the way he pulls on the bars and so forth. If he's experienced, though, he's going to conceal everything.

When a rider starts having a jerky pedal rhythm, he's getting ready to blow up and you know you can finish him off for sure. But what you want to do is get somebody sooner than that point. You want to be able to tell a little bit earlier whether it's time to extend yourself or not.

WHAT TO DO IF THE BREAK GETS CAUGHT

It happens sometimes that there is just one breakaway in a race. The field may continue to attack sporadically but nothing gets together.

If your break is getting caught, keep riding and maybe a new group will form.

Normally, however, there are two or three groups going. There are probably enough good riders left in the field who realize after the first break goes what they have to do. A leader or organizer might get ten guys each to take a 150-yard pull, so that the field is really moving. They might even break into a second group automatically.

If you feel your breakaway is going to get caught and don't have enough starch to go on your own, don't drop back to the field. Never wait for them; make them catch you. Just ride along and keep it going, but don't coast. Don't go so hard that you go sour, of course, but keep it moving. The reason for this is that if you stay out there a few riders may break away from the field to join you and then you're on your way again.

57

I've often seen it happen that, when the field catches a break-away, the chasers in the field have used up almost everything. The break, then a few chasers, then the field are all making contact at once. It's like a rubber band that stretches and then goes back together.

Suddenly maybe two or three riders will go off the front again. They may not be the same riders who were out there before, but perhaps a few of them are. This new break has a good chance of success because the field is already tired. If you stretch the rubber band far enough, in other words, it will snap.

GETTING AWAY FROM A BREAKAWAY

Getting away from a break is usually pretty difficult, depending on who's in it. If you are in a breakaway with several riders who can beat you in the sprint, you can try to get away from them before the line. If you know your own fitness pretty well, for example, three or four miles from the finish, perhaps going up a small grade, you can attack and get a gap. Stay out there for two miles and make them work very hard in chasing. When they catch you with maybe a mile to go, look like you've really had it. But this attack was a phoney, and you still have something left.

Although you made them work very hard, you should still have just a little reserve and hopefully they have less. Just dangle in the back while they keep it going and then at the right moment, maybe with a half a mile to go, hit it again and come by.

THE SPRINT FINISH

Road sprinting lacks the explosiveness of track sprinting. It winds up faster and faster but there is no jump or snap as there would be on the track.

A downhill sprint is generally difficult to win from the front. It's better to take a rush from the rear. If there's a headwind it's also difficult to win from the front.

If there's a tailwind, that's the time to take a flyer. Make an attack and try to get two or three lengths. If you have any speed at all, it's hard for the group to catch up, because in a tailwind they don't have as much of your slipstream to shoot at.

An uphill finish can go either way. It can be good to go from the front if you're accelerating all the way to the line, but you can't go too long. If you do go too long, they're going to take a shot off your wheel and pass.

Make your move as close to the line as possible but remember that when it gets within striking distance someone else is going to go, too. Four hundred yards is a good place if you have a strong sprint, because the other riders usually haven't gotten going by then. They will wait until 150 yards if it's uphill or into a headwind. Even in a good tailwind they may not be on their way until 250-300 yards.

Before the sprint starts, get ready by being in the gear that you want to sprint in. If it's going to finish on the top of a hill you might go to a lower gear, but usually you go to a slightly larger gear than that used when doing your riding or pacing.

In most road finishes you get out of the saddle in the early part of the sprint to get the extra momentum going. Then, if the gear is the right one, and you get it going fast enough, you can sit down and pedal it up some more. If the gear is too big, you're going to have to stand on it all the way to the end. Of course, if it's a short sprint, you may want to stand on it to the end in order to be accelerating all the way. But riding out of the saddle becomes inefficient. After you get your rpm's up to a certain point it's better to sit down and pedal it up.

Occasionally riders start their jump in one gear and then hit a bigger gear halfway through the sprint. They'll make their jump, get it going, and sit down for awhile, but if that gear doesn't feel good, they'll hit another one and maybe get out of the seat again.

You might lose a split second shifting during the sprint, but it can be done quite quickly. You can still be moving, because all you're doing is dropping from one cog to a smaller one on the back. It just clunks in. If you had to shift from a small cog to a large one, though, you'd lose a lot of time, because the derailleur mechanism doesn't shift up as easily as it shifts down.

A lead-out from a teammate can be a big help at the finish. In a lead-out one rider sacrifices himself to break the wind for someone else coming into the sprint. Often the two will split the prize afterwards.

Your teammate might go at about 350 yards from the line. Don't sit right on his wheel, because then you'd have to go around him. Let him get one or two lengths ahead, leaving a dead air space to rush into when you make your move. These two lengths of slipstream will create a slingshot effect, giving lots of momentum before you have to come by him out in the wind.

Be very attentive and careful to protect the space behind your lead-out man and not let someone else into it. If you see a wheel coming up beside you, it is time to close the gap.

The lead-out doesn't have to be from the front position. Your teammate might be in second and you might be in third, coming into the sprint. He can peel out from the leader at about 275 yards to go and then you pass at about 100 yards. This is something you can practice on training rides.

There is always a tendency to make mistakes in the sprint, whether it's going too early or waiting too long. You have to know the circumstances, know your opponents, know yourself, and make the right decisions. Going too early is the same as going too late. It doesn't help you to win.

SAFETY AND SPORTSMANSHIP

Safety in racing is very important. Watch out for the others and they'll watch out for you.

When cornering, for example, especially in a big field, you should be concerned with not crashing. If you're right in the middle of a bunch of riders, just follow through. If you're a beginner, don't take chances and try to improve your position, because you won't get anything out of the race if you crash.

Timing is important in the sprint finish and if there is enough distance left to the line, the second rider may move up through the
lead rider's slipstream and win.

This is where a lot of riders make a mistake. They don't realize
that the most important thing is staying upright and not falling
down. Never fight for wheels or position because there is always
time left in the race. Ride for safety, because it's not going to do
you any good to wind up on the pavement. Nobody ever wins
prizes or jerseys or medals or gets on Olympic teams by lying on
the ground.

As far as sportsmanship is concerned, anything goes, but you
have to be ready for the consequences. There are no holds barred

61

when it comes to winning; you just do what you have to do. For example, a rider might be away with a break and can't pull through. He promises the other riders that if they let him hang in there he won't sprint. Then if he does sprint at the end, perhaps because there's a big prize, he should realize what they might do to him the next time.

Some people complain if there is a rider hanging on to the break and not taking his pull. They accuse him of wheel-sucking or sleigh riding, as if this were unsportsmanlike. But it's up to you to go hard enough to get rid of that guy, and if you can't then you just have to make the best of it.

Drop him or hold him in and attack him or do whatever you have to do, but don't accuse him of being a leech. He may be drafting, but he's still hanging in there, and he's riding the best race he knows how.

INDIVIDUAL STYLE

After a few seasons of racing, you will start to see where your talents lie and what kinds of racing you are good at.

Use the tactics that are best suited to your own style. If you're a sprinter, wait for the end. If you're a hill climber, try to force the pace on the hills. If you're slow but very strong, then attack, attack, attack.

An all-'rounder can play it by ear, going with the break if it looks like a good break or waiting for the sprint, too. If there are no really good sprinters in the field, or you know you can beat them, then you want it to come to a sprint at the end.

If you're a good pursuer, then three or four miles from the end might be the time to go. Maybe even fifteen miles from the end if it's flat ground.

When you start excelling in certain fields and realize you have certain strengths, develop them. But besides your strengths, you must also work on your weaknesses, which is what a lot of riders don't do.

One well-known road rider is a good example of someone who could have been much better if he had worked on his weaknesses. He had lots of endurance but no speed, excelling at stage racing but almost always placing last in any final sprint.

This rider should have worked on speed in his training and in his racing, too. He should have sat down to think, "What am I lacking?" He should have made a point of doing some weekly track racing and when he went to the track he should have asked himself, "What kind of mental attitude do I have to have to do this kind of racing?"

Think what this man could have done if he had developed some kind of a sprint. It means the difference between first and tenth place. It's as simple as that.

chapter five

THE RACING KIT

If the race is on a Sunday, on Saturday evening you should go over the whole bike to make sure it's ready. Check that the tires are properly cemented on, the handlebars tight, and the gears working smoothly. Anything that will be inspected on the line should be double-checked before you get there.

Your bike should be clean. Some people claim this doesn't matter, but a clean bike doesn't have anything extra on it. It's ready to race and it makes you feel ready, too.

Preparing your racing kit either the night before or the morning of the race, it's a good idea to lay the stuff out on your bed and have a check list in mind to make sure you don't forget

road racing

anything. The first thing to remember is your bike shoes. They are the most personal thing you have for riding since they attach you to the bicycle.

You should always take two pairs of tights. The spare pair is in case you have a crash or rip a pair or get a hole in them, or even just in case your teammate forgets his tights. Take the jersey you're going to race in, an extra jersey, and a wool undervest to put on while warming up. Since you're never sure of the weather conditions, take a long-sleeved jersey and a pair of leg warmers for warming up also. Put in your helmet and sponsor's cap, if you have one, plus racing gloves, socks, and so on.

The food to take with you depends on what kind of race it is. Eat your last meal about three hours before the race, but if the

Before or after the race, it's important to look presentable. Ron Skarin helps the sport by being neat and courteous as he talks to interviewers.

race is 50 miles or more, you might want to bring along a jelly sandwich and a thermos of tea to eat half an hour before the race. It's not necessary to carry food during a short race.

Pack a brush, a couple of wash mitts, and a towel if you want to shower after the race. If you can't take a shower you'll need cologne or rubbing alcohol to clean off with.

Right after you're finished racing and before you get your prize, always slip on a clean dry jersey. It's important to look presentable when you go up to the stand. It's part of the image and it helps the sport with the public and with sponsors.

66

Professional riders give sponsors their money's worth by appearing clean, well-dressed, and proud of their uniform.

A ripped jersey, floppy dirty socks, or unshaved face and legs are not a good advertisement for cycling. If you love the sport you will want to make a good impression on the public and the sponsors by a neat clean appearance. It's **great** to be an individual and do your own thing, but sponsors and promoters are people who treat the sport as a business and they want their workers to be businesslike. American riders who have gone to Europe have learned this overseas, where everybody wants to get a pro contract. Even in a tiny little criterium, every bum comes to the race looking like a banker because he knows maybe that's going to mean the difference between some kind of a contract or not.

A good position at the start can prevent accidents.

All the tools should fit in a little satchel. You need a tool for everything on the bike; an allen key for the sprocket, a hub wrench, a seat wrench, an allen key for the handlebar stem, a six-inch adjustable wrench, a spoke wrench, cone wrenches, a chain breaker, brake cables, a pair of pliers, and also a cluster remover if you don't have spare wheels.

If you do forget something, it's annoying at first but try to overcome it. Things are going to go wrong all your life in everything you do—not only in racing, but especially in racing—and to really get ahead you should make the best of any situation and not let it bother you. Try your best not to forget anything, but if you do forget something, all right, allow yourself the luxury of being annoyed for a few minutes and then get on to the business at hand.

THE START

Get to the race at least an hour early and, after signing in and getting your number, go out and ride around the course to test your equipment. Make sure the bike is ready and eliminate that one small thing that can cost you the race. Attention to these details sometimes pays off.

Ride in a comfortable gear for about 15 or 20 minutes, checking out the bicycle and looking over the course. By the time of the start you should be warmed up, but certainly not sweating profusely. Rather, you should feel warm and loosened up, but also fresh.

Look at the prize sheet to see what primes there are so you can anticipate when there might be a breakaway. When you get your

If a break goes early, the front riders have an advantage.

number, look at the list of riders and their numbers and try to remember which numbers to watch.

Try to get as good a position on the line as possible and just before the start you can sometimes move up a few rows by riding along the curb on the outside of the field. Try to be right at the front to eliminate any chance of crashing. You could easily have an accident before the first turn that might take you out of the race.

You also have to be prepared for a quick breakaway. If the good riders are going to force the pace very early, the whole field could snap right in the middle immediately. Sometimes the good riders will go right to the front, force the pace, and set up an echelon. There will be an echelon, then a string of riders behind, and if the string snaps the echelon will go off by itself, leaving the other riders floundering in the back. Even though they eventually set up their own echelon, the front one usually has the best riders in it so it's going faster. That's why you should be up there where things are going on.

HAVE A PLAN

The mental attitude for entering a bicycle race is not very different from any other sport. Don't get too up-tight before the race, at least not until about five minutes before the start, because that drains your energy. But you do have to have a plan for the race.

The plan is not something you're going to follow by the book. You have to play it by ear, whatever happens. It's like a sprinter who comes to the line for a match sprint with several different stock plans of what's going to happen. If his opponent does such-and-such he knows what he's going to do, and if the opponent does something else, then he knows what he has to do in return. He doesn't really have to think about it, he just does it.

So keep the possibilities in mind. A good sprinter might say, "I'm going for the prize at the end; I'm not going to go for any primes; I'm going to go with anything that looks like a good break, and when we get to the end I'm going for the win." A strong road rider may force the pace throughout the race and then figure, "Okay, I'm going to make my attack with three or four laps to go and ride alone to the end." An all-'rounder might have three or four plans.

FEEDING AND "THE BONK"

Except in a very short race, you must drink liquid during an event; this is carried in a water bottle on the bike or in a back pocket of the racing jersey.

Liquid is important because the body is much more efficient when operating in its normal temperature range. If you continually consume liquids, taking on a little bit at a time, you're operating probably about two degrees lower than if you let yourself get into a condition of dehydration. So keep sipping when you can and you will perform much more efficiently. If it's very hot, for example, you might use two bottles of fluid in fifty miles.

There are a number of replacement drinks that contain some

Plain water is the best liquid to take because you can also pour it over your head on a hot day.

of the substances lost in perspiration. These are good but they can leave a saccharine taste in the mouth. Some people like water with a little bit of lemon. Some people take tea during a race, but if you spill this on yourself it's sticky. That's why I feel plain water is the best. You can do everything with it. If it's hot you can sprinkle it over your head or your feet or your neck.

If a race lasts more than 70-75 miles, you may also need to eat at about the 40-mile point. Your body wears down like a battery. Ask any cyclist what it's like to run out of energy in a race; you get what they call "the bonk." You pedal in triangles and see black spots in front of your eyes. This comes from not eating, and you can prevent it by training for the event properly and by taking food after a certain amount of time.

Fruit is good to eat during a race because fruits have salts and other things that you lose in sweat. Carbohydrates are necessary, too. They're like firewood—instant energy. I wouldn't recommend eating anything that has a lot of acid.

Bananas are a favorite. Raisins are difficult to digest. Things that have skins on them, like apples, you should peel and cut up. A lot of people like oranges because they clean out the mucus

72

and the buildup in your mouth, but other people can't eat oranges because they're too acid. Riders also carry sandwiches made of honey or cheese or other concoctions. It all depends on the individual.

As soon as you feel the slightest bit hungry, you should definitely eat something. After a while you'll learn how long you can ride until you start feeling bad; you should eat just before this happens so you won't go through any period of weakness.

In training you can actually change your metabolism. I've found that if I'm sprinting regularly and then try to start training for a long-distance event, I'll start to get that weak feeling after two and a half hours. But as I train over a period of time, I can go longer and longer without getting that. I believe your metabolism adapts to the event you are training for. A sprinter has to consume his energy in eleven seconds. He burns it up immediately and his metabolism is geared to that. So when a sprinter goes on a road ride his metabolism is working faster and it utilizes the food he has eaten in a shorter period of time.

Even famous riders get the bonk if they don't eat and go out riding. It's not a thing to be ashamed of. It's just a fact; if you don't eat any food you're not going to have anything to burn.

There is a funny thing that happens, though. Let's say you get stuck out on the road with no money and no food, or you're in a race and didn't get fed. You'll go through a super-weak period, but if you can get through that then you seem to come back again a little bit. I think this is when your body begins to utilize fat reserves. Even a very fit athlete still has over ten percent fat. So you definitely experience some kind of revitalization.

FEEDING TECHNIQUE

Originally it was difficult to get to the places on the course to feed riders. This is why there were pockets in the front of the jerseys, to carry more food. But now a lot of the races aren't that long, the roads are better, and riders can carry most of what they need in their rear pockets.

Whether to carry all your food with you or pick it up along the way depends on how long the race is, how many feeding stations there are, and whether you can depend on people to feed you.

If you have complete faith in the people who are working for you, and their job is to be there at the feeding zone, then it's nice not to carry the weight. You know for sure that you can get fed along the way. Perhaps your trainer explains the route and says, "This is where we're going to feed you." He'll have everything ready and you won't have all that bulk in your jersey.

But in a smaller event without so much support, it's better to carry your own food. In a lot of races you're not really sure what's going on and the people who work for you are not really sure what's going on and nobody knows the course. So you should carry as much as you can.

Feeding is usually done at a place on the course where the race isn't going very fast. It might be just at the crest of a little grade, for example. It can be difficult to get fed if the riders are bunched together when they come into the feeding area, so you should try to spread out a little. Sometimes you will see riders grabbing for other people's food, or even trying to knock other people's food to the ground.

It's always a good idea to plan out what you do, whether it's the race itself or the feeding. If you decide beforehand to be fed on the left side of the road, then you'll only have to look to the left. Your trainer could wear a certain color jersey—pure white or pure red—or use a yellow musette bag or the team colors. All that is helpful.

To hand up a water bottle, your trainer should place his fingers around the neck and hold it from the top, then run along with it, looking where he is going. For instance, if he is on the right side of the road he should hold the bottle in his left hand and glance over his left shoulder. He trots along and you just come by and pluck it right out of his hand. The trainer should be sure to hold the bottle steady and to watch out that other people don't grab it or knock it down.

Food is handed up in a musette bag, a square cloth bag with a

The trainer holds the water bottle by the neck and runs along until the rider plucks it out of his hand.

long loop. The trainer holds the loop out and you must stick your arm through it and throw it around your back as you come by. It's not necessary to run with the musette bag; it's just held.

However you do it, feeding is important in the race. A water bottle is a lifeline and even an apple tastes like a feast when you've been out there for a long time.

HOW TO KEEP GOING

If there is another race the next day and they have no chance of getting a prize, many professional riders will not finish an event.

Musette bags are used to hand up food to riders during a long race.

But if there are no more races for a few days or if you are unfit and need the training, then by all means continue just for the miles. Racing is one of the very best forms of training. Also when you are a beginner it may be important for you to be able to say, "I did it; I finished the race."

A good thing to do, if you're feeling like quitting but still want to go as far as possible, is to set a certain goal for yourself. Tell yourself that you're only going to continue until a certain landmark, or that you're only going to ride another five minutes. Often at the end of the five minutes you can tell yourself, "I got here. I'm just going another five minutes and then that's all. I'll get out; I've had enough for today; I can't do it." You can go on and on and on like that.

I learned this when I was seventeen and riding in the Olympic Games in Rome as a sprinter. There was another young fellow there, a road rider, and we went out for a training ride to the sea and back. It must have been a distance of about sixty miles round trip and I had never ridden more than thirty miles at one time before.

On the way back the other rider, who was always making bets, said, "Let's race to the velodrome side by side for a ten thousand lire prize." So I said, "That sounds like fun," and off we went side by side.

I didn't know where we were or how far from the track, but he did. Eventually we got to within one mile of it, but I didn't realize that and thought we had another 25 miles to go. He knew that once I saw the track I would beat him because I was a sprinter. We came to a place in the road where the track was about three hundred yards down the left fork and he said, "Let's take the right fork." He thought I knew where the track was and that by telling me to go the other way it was showing how strong he was. Meanwhile I was saying to myself, "Oh man, I'm going to quit; I can't go on." So I told myself, "I'm going to go to that telephone pole up there and when we get there I'm going to tell him that I'm finished."

We kept going and got to that telephone pole and I was hurting really bad, but I said, "No, I'm going to go him one more telephone pole." And halfway to the next telephone pole he said, "I quit. You win." He couldn't go any farther. That goes to show that when you feel bad the others probably feel the same way. So sometimes if you can set yourself marks like that, it helps.

DON'T GET DISCOURAGED

It's always a good idea to go into each race with the attitude that you're going to win; but of course not everybody can do that. When you're a beginning cyclist, though, you can still set yourself a certain goal and try to carry it out.

The beginner is going to try to see if he can stay with the field. He's going to try to get to know the other riders. He's going to see riders who are just a little bit better than he is and after a while he'll try to stay with them and beat them at the end.

Take one step at a time, but always have a goal, because there's not that much racing in this country that you can use races just for training. Perhaps the best place to start is in fairly flat events, where a beginner has a better chance of staying with the field. Go into these races for your own benefit, to start getting used to the faster tempo.

With the institution of Junior World Championships, events in this class have become more competitive than ever.

You have to realize that the better riders are not going to want you in the race with them. First, they want the prizes for themselves; second, as a beginner, your riding may be shaky and dangerous. The better riders might go especially hard trying to drop you. To undermine your confidence they may try to browbeat you verbally. Pay no mind to this. Even if the race is going hard, just try to hang on as long as possible without being erratic or dangerous. Try to ride smoothly and with courage and maybe you can come in for a place or a prize somewhere.

After racing a little bit, if you are strong and picking it up fast, try an attack off the front just to see what it feels like. You don't have to have the idea of carrying through to the end, because if you get absorbed you must still have enough left to hang in the field. But you must also test yourself.

Don't get discouraged by poor performances in the beginning because, like anything else, it takes a lot of race savvy and knowing what you're doing as well as developing yourself physically to perform well. The old timers say that it takes five years to make a good bike rider. Maybe it doesn't take that long, but I think it does take a few seasons.

chapter six

THE CRITERIUM

A beginning rider should enter as many different kinds of races as he can, to gain experience and to find out what he enjoys and what he is good at. Perhaps the best single kind of race in which to find where your ability lies is the criterium, because in it there is something for everyone. Everything that you do in bike racing can be brought out in a criterium. You can find out if you have a sprint, you can find out what kind of endurance you have, and it teaches you bike handling. It is a blend of road and track racing.

What is a Criterium?

A criterium is a short flat road race held on a closed circuit that

road events

measures less than two miles around. Because it is usually held on city streets, the course is most often rectangular. Common race distances are from 25 miles up to 100 kilometers (62 miles), which can mean as many as 100 laps. The criterium is a popular way to promote racing in America because it passes the spectators often—every two or three minutes—which makes it more exciting. Also, it doesn't take up the whole day, as a 100-mile road race can. Criteriums may be held annually by towns in conjunction with local festivities.

Frequent primes make a criterium different from a road race because there is something happening all the time. For instance, if there is a prime on every lap, then every time you cross the line some rider is trying for a prize because that's his thing in the

Held on short closed courses, criteriums are very popular with both spectators and riders.

race. Everybody is doing his own thing, but they are also all coming together at the end to try to win the race.

A lot of riders who can't last the distance will enter a criterium just to go for the primes. If they're still hanging in there at the end, fine, but they may shoot their entire wad just to get a prime prize.

When I was riding as an amateur, there was one well-known fifty-mile criterium that had a big prime at the 25-mile mark. At about the 23-mile mark suddenly all the sprinters would go to the front and nobody could get away. Then at 25 miles there would be a big sprint and the winner of that, nine times out of ten, would be sitting on the curb eating ice cream and watching the race on the next lap.

Big prizes do make a race go faster. It's nice to ride for the sport and for the glory of winning, but it makes you feel more worthwhile if you are also getting some kind of compensation. Riders spend a lot of time training and a lot of money on equipment, and they will train harder and sacrifice more if they know they can get something back. This makes criteriums popular with riders because all types of riders have a chance to come away with a prize.

The major primes are published with the race entry or program and a bell is rung one lap before each one, just as it is for the finish of the race. However, spectators sometimes come to the announcer's stand and put up merchandise for a prime during the race. If there is a public address system the announcer will broadcast this and the bell will ring with one lap to go. It does occasionally happen that riders lose track of the primes, so it pays to be alert or to have a helper stationed along the course to let you know what is going on.

A criterium is a very general kind of race because it encompasses everything in the sport. There's something there for a sprinter and there's something there for a road rider. Everybody can compete at a more equal level than in a road race or in a match sprint.

What Makes a Good Criterium Rider?

You definitely have to have speed in your legs to be a good criterium rider. There is a lot of accelerating out of every turn and even in the pack the speed is very fast. A sluggish rider who can pound along all day against the wind and the elements but doesn't have that turn of speed is not going to fare well. Quick reflexes are also needed because everybody's close together and there's a lot of turning, especially if there is a figure-eight course.

Either a road rider who has a good sprint or a track rider who has some staying ability should be good at this type of racing. A strong sprinter is excellent because he has the quickness and the reflexes and he's cagey, too. Or a fast road rider often wins, if he's very versatile. An all-'rounder will win more criteriums than the guy who can just sprint or the guy who can flog everybody to death.

Equipment

Although the most important thing in the race is pushing the

83

A winning streak of four races in a row earned Wayne Stetina the
title in the National Prestige Championship, an annual criterium
series.

bike, high-quality equipment does help. It's a little thing, but I believe that if you are going to do something you should do it the right way or at least as well as you can.

Since a criterium is an all-around type of race, most people won't be bothered with changing their saddle position or putting another stem on their bike just for one race. Everyone just uses his regular road bike and it's easy to adapt.

However, if you do have a choice of bicycles, it's really nice in a criterium to ride a bike with a high bottom bracket. You can get an extra pedal stroke going into and coming out of the turns, which means a lot. If the race is really moving, you can get a length ahead on every corner because you can keep on going when the other riders have to start slowing down. If you have a bike that's hitting the pedal, like a road bike with a low bottom bracket, it can be very discouraging.

Most people don't have a criterium bike, but I've found it can be a real help, especially when the race is fast. I once had a bicycle with such a high bottom bracket that I could pedal all the way through the turns and get five lengths on the field before they even stopped coasting. Although a bike like that can be a little less stable than a road bike because of the higher center of gravity, the fact that you can pedal farther is more advantageous.

Wheels are important, too, when doing so much cornering. It's a good idea to ride stiff wheels in criteriums. They shouldn't be the lightest wheels in the world, because they have to take a lot of punishment in those turns. A wheel that's not stiff can make you wobble and give you an uneasy feeling; a wheel that flexes in the turn can throw you out of line. In a criterium race, where a lot of riders are going into the turn all packed together, this kind of thing might cause a pile-up.

Road wheels with cross-three spokes and low flange hubs can be used on very bumpy or cobblestoned courses. But in general for a criterium, ride a stiffer heavier wheel with 36 spokes, cross-three or cross-four, and high flange hubs. This is as opposed to, say, 28 spokes, cross-three, and light rims. Of course, people have proved that you can win races without the stiffer wheel.

Having a high bottom bracket can enable you to pedal through a turn and gain distance on your competitors.

Usually three gears are enough in a criterium unless it is very windy, but you do have to be prepared for all conditions. A popular cluster setup on the back is 14 through 18, although some riders use 13-17 or even 13-18 if they have a six-gear cluster. On the front some go as high as a 55-chain ring, but in most cases the races in this country never go faster than the need for a 52 or 53.

Tires depend on the road surfaces. If it's a super-clean road surface, you can get away with 185- or 195-gram tires. If you are not sure about the road surface, 250s are always very safe to ride. If it's only a little bit dirty, maybe you can get away with 220s. They will hold up but still be fast.

One thing I've learned, however, is not to take a chance with equipment; be safe. If you have to go to a tiny bit heavier tire, go ahead. I've had flats riding very light tires and wasn't able to get back in the field. In criteriums it's particularly difficult because they're moving very fast all the time and if you get off the back a certain distance, it's hard to get back in. In most criteriums lapped riders are pulled out of the race, unless they are still in contention for a prize.

The proper tires are very important in the rain. Ride something with a bit of tread on it, such as honeycomb or file pattern. For some reason, red tires seem to slip more, so whenever it rains you see riders taking off their red tires or changing their wheels.

On a dry day with a clean road surface, you can put about 8 or 9 atmospheres pressure in your tires. But if it rains or is bumpy, you want your tires somewhat softer—about 6 atmospheres.

Tactics in the Criterium

Basically the same tactics apply in a criterium as in any other road race, but the primes and frequent corners do provide special opportunities for riders to break away. Tactics also become more complex because of the fact that there are several types of riders.

A pure sprinter might just go into the race to get some primes or he might use it for training and just sit in the field. He might say, "If there's a bunch sprint then I'm going to get worked up for the end."

If a sprinter wants to win he knows he has to get to the end, so he has to conserve every bit of energy. He may not go for any primes and probably won't join a solo break either. But when he sees a good larger group develop he'll go out and get it. With three or four riders, he can sit in the back longer because he only has to take a turn at the front every fourth or fifth time. With only two other riders, he'd have to take his turn every third man, which would be hard for him.

If the sprinter wants to win the race and three riders get away who are all good and strong and going well, he's got to make his mind up immediately. He's either going to go with them and suffer to the end or he's going to sit there and not win the race.

A road rider is just the opposite. When the gun goes off, he certainly shouldn't wait long before attacking—and he'll probably want to force the pace from the beginning. One well-known road rider won quite a few criteriums just by putting it in a great big gear, getting ten yards off the front, and forcing everyone to catch him again and again. By the time he'd done it fifty times he'd tired out everyone else. You have to know your opponents and know what kind of a race is best for you.

In a criterium you can often use the wind in your breakaway attempt. Perhaps there is a headwind going into a certain turn and the field will not be moving too fast. Attack going into the corner, and you will go through the whole turn faster than they're moving. You come out faster, too, while they really haven't had a chance to get going. As soon as you come out onto the tailwind straightaway, the wind hits and starts blowing you away. With a tailwind you can really go fast by yourself; it's almost like sitting in. By this time the field may get moving, but you are still out there and have gotten the gap.

If the course is a figure eight or a very small rectangle, it is possible to get completely out of sight of the field. There is something to the saying, "Out of sight, out of mind." If they can always look up and see you, they figure they can drag you in little by little and wear you down. Just because they can keep looking at you, they have something to gauge it by. But once out of sight, you're on equal terms; you start getting confidence. They can't see you and their minds are not always directed on you.

An important aspect in criterium racing is being able to pedal through the turn. When you're coasting you're slowing down, you're not accelerating. Pedal as far in as you can, make the widest arc possible in order to go through the fastest, and pedal as soon as you can afterwards. As soon as you get out, pedal; don't wait.

If it's a race that's really moving, you might be out of the saddle on each turn. You should expect this and be prepared to make a jump out of every corner.

When you consider that there may be at least one hundred corners in a 25-mile criterium, it is obvious that each extra length you gain here will add up.

It's all right to be a specialist, but I think you have to be able to ride everything to be a good cyclist. The criterium, with its speed and activity, is a race in which everybody can be competitive and this makes it one of the best all-'round tests of riding ability.

THE ROAD RACE
Courses and Equipment

Although a criterium is technically a road race, the latter term usually applies to an event that is held on quite a large circuit. A road race could be run on an out-and-back or even a point-to-point course. Ninety percent of these courses naturally have some hills in them, although not necessarily. There is no set distance for a road race, but they generally are 100 kilometers or longer.

A big difference between a longer road race and a criterium is that, except for very important events, the course is not usually closed. Sometimes the promoter arranges to close certain sections of the course from one point to another as the race progresses,

Courses for longer road races are not usually closed.

but often it is not closed at all. Many states in this country frown on bicycle road racing because it disrupts traffic. In California, I believe, the riders must come to a complete halt and put one foot on the ground at every stop sign.

Even in Europe, the center of the sport, the automobile is really pressing on road racing. A lot of the big races are being cut down or rerouted because of the auto. A world road champion was killed in a race in Belgium when he crossed the center line and was hit by a car coming in the other direction. Of course, this doesn't happen often, but increased accidents and traffic are contributing factors in the decline of road racing overseas.

Although criteriums are a popular first race for beginners in

90

many parts of the country and there are some who ride nothing but criteriums all season, I think a new rider should start in the first race that comes along. There are several reasons why a road race is a good way to begin.

In a criterium, fast reflexes and experience are necessary because everyone is bunched so tightly together and moving so fast. A regular road race has less turning and less bunching up, so it can be a safer and more satisfying race for a beginner. Best of all, perhaps, is a handicap road race, where the beginners will be first off the line and the other riders will try to catch them. Years ago in the area where I live the first race of the season was always a 50-mile handicap.

As a rider develops himself, he gets a built-in pacemaker that will show him the speed he can go for different distances. In a road race, though, you are not competing by yourself. Others around you are setting the pace. It goes fast; it goes slow; and often you have to go along with the pace of someone else. A road race is not the sort of event where you can go out and say, "Well, I have a hundred miles to do and I realize I can't go any faster than this, or I feel this is as hard as I can go." Sometimes you have to go like the finish is 200 yards down the road. You can't think about the end.

In a road race you use the same equipment as in training, except for slightly lighter wheels and tires—if you have them and if the road surface is suitable. In a fairly flat road race, you might put 48 and 53 chain rings on the front with a 14-through-18 cluster on the back. But if it's hilly, a wider variety of gears is needed. You might use a 42 with a 53 or 54 on the front. I have two six-speed clusters that I use in road races: a 13-14-15-17-19-21 and, for very hilly races, a 14-15-16-18-20-22.

Make the Most of the Hills

Since there are more hills in a road race than in a criterium, it is important to know how to conserve energy when climbing. Get toward the front if you are in a large field coming into the hill.

As you start climbing, let the rest of the riders drift by you little by little. You will be going up the hill more slowly but, since you started at the front, you'll only be three-quarters of the way back when you get to the top. You'll save energy by not going at the same speed and also you'll get a little wind protection. This technique is a real basic of racing.

Because the riders are not moving as fast uphill, there is very little wind protection from just sitting in the field, so a good hill climber can often ride right off the front. If you can force yourself to do this, it will blow everyone else off because they can't draft.

A sprinter can go up a short hill much faster than a road rider because of his tremendous power. But when the hill gets longer the lightest riders with the best cardiovascular fitness will be able to ride away. There is hardly any power involved at all; they just twiddle right up the hill.

It is common for new riders to slow up after they've made any kind of effort. They think they're going to rest and they subconsciously sit up higher on the bike and relax. You can see them do this at the top of a hill. But in a race there's no rest; there's pressure all the time. You don't slow up when you go over the top. As a matter of fact, as soon as you hit the top you should go right into your larger range, your larger chain ring. Get off the saddle a little bit to stretch your muscles and accelerate.

THE TIME TRIAL

A time trial is a race against the clock and, done right, it can be as hard as any event in cycling. It's an exercise of fitness and concentration. Time trials can be over any distance or space of time. There are twenty-four-hour time trials and 25-mile time trials. There are even time trials on the track that last about one minute.

The Individual Time Trial

In an individual road time trial, the riders usually start one minute apart; the start and finish times are recorded and used to find the overall time for the distance. The man ahead of you is called your minute man and it does provide some incentive to try to catch him. Most time trials, including championship events, are held on out-and-back courses with a 180-degree turn at the end, but they can also be run point-to-point.

Road time trial specialists reveal that the key to this event is developing the strength and endurance to push a big gear for sustained effort. The best American riders consistently time trial in a 53-13. If you push a bigger gear than you're used to in a time trial and think you're going slow because it hurts, don't worry. You have to push yourself even beyond the point where you think it's effective.

Pacing is important and the tempo should be a little bit faster than you think you can maintain for the whole distance. Break your ride into segments by going to the turn-around as if it were the finish and then say, "I'm half done. I can do it." There is no resting. It's just a total effort and you never can tell how you've done until you finish. Sometimes you think you did great and you're terrible. Other times you think you're not going fast enough and you win.

A streamlined position is important, with the hands on the hooks or sometimes on the top of the brake levers. Some riders like a slightly higher and more forward position than usual since there is a tendency to slide forward in an all-out effort. The time trial is the place to use light equipment if you have it.

According to the experts, your stomach should be practically empty so that you feel very light when you come to the start. Next to hill climbing, a time trial is the most likely place for a rider to throw up, since it is such a tremendous strain and effort.

No matter what the distance, you have to start fast. You don't want to spend the first miles warming up, so you should be more thoroughly warmed up than is usual for a road race. Roll an hour in low gears or go fast; you must find out for yourself what is the best way to prepare.

At the start and during the ride, concentrate on breathing deeply. A lot of coaches in endurance sports stress deep breath-

Junior time trial champion Paul Deem practiced his start many many times to learn deep breathing and rapid acceleration.

ing exercises since there is a tendency in hard effort to breathe quickly and shallowly, or pant. It takes concentration to counteract this. You can tell you are breathing deeply if, when you lie on your back in bed and put a hand on your stomach, it rises up and down when you breathe.

Get over the hills in the biggest gear you can, as long as you don't die or slow down at the top. On short steep hills you don't want to lose speed by having to shift gears. People tend to relax on the downhills so this is a good place to make up time. Throw it into your biggest gear and keep it rolling. Let your gears work for you.

(Facing page) Time trial champion Mary Jane Reoch shows the all-out effort and streamlined position needed for this against-the-clock event.

An Olympic and World Championship event, the 100-kilometer time trial is for four-man teams. The riders start together and take turns at the front.

The Team Time Trial

Where stamina and strength are necessary for the individual time trialist, a team time trial rider must also have speed on the pedals. Although he rides the same gears as the individual, he has to turn the cranks faster. The team time trial is pure speed and recovery.

Team time trials can consist of two, three, four, or theoretically any number of riders on a team. The teams usually start more than a minute apart, perhaps five or ten, and each man takes turns at the front. No one gets a rest, but the switching off does make a breakup of the effort. Time in a four-man team event is usually taken on the front wheel of the third man, so it is not always necessary for the entire team to finish.

The exact pattern of riding and switching off depends on the

Frequent World Champions in the team trial, the Swedes are well-matched and strong, working smoothly together.

coach, but each man has a certain number of revolutions of the crank to pull at the front, usually about twenty. As in an individual time trial, there's not too much you can do to win except go fast and cut corners. It's important to know the course and to plan what gears to use in different places.

As in an echelon, the riders pull off into the wind after their turn at the front. It is very important to be smooth and not lose time in these changes. On the top teams everyone is equally matched and each does an equal share. If there is a weaker rider he should be coached to take a shorter pull at the front if he is slowing down the pace. Having a weak man does put a kink in things, though, because the other riders get less rest. Even a strong man can crack unexpectedly. He may blow just from nerves or some other reason, such as sickness or bad morale.

In time trial events, the very best road men almost always

Stage races can cover hundreds of miles over several days or weeks. Total time determines the winner.

place well and the training involves the same elements as regular mass start road racing. Since time trialing is a championship event and many stage races are won and lost in the time trial stage, it is worthwhile spending some time cultivating this skill.

STAGE RACING

A stage race is a series of races in which the final time of each event is added up to determine the winner, who is the rider with the least time. The stages themselves can be criteriums, time trials, or road races. Time bonuses can be given for primes or for the first few positions in the finish of a certain stage in order to make the riders try hard in the final meters each day. There are often team prizes.

Many stage races in this country involve only two or three events on a weekend, but the bigger international ones last several weeks and cover as much as a thousand miles in that time. The most famous bicycle race in the world, the Tour de France, is a three-week stage race for professionals.

It definitely takes experience to ride stage races because of the tremendous effort day after day. I think you have to ride a couple of them to realize that you're even capable of doing it. If you're always around riders who compete in stage races, perhaps a lot could rub off through conversation and you might know what to expect and how to train for it. But if you went into one stone-cold, I think it would shock you. You ride one day and you're tired, and then you ride the next day and you're more tired, and then you have to ride again and again and again. You don't realize you can do this, but you can.

Much of anyone's success in a stage race depends on his support team. If you have no support, forget it. There's not a rider in the world who can do well in a stage race if he hasn't the right support.

You shouldn't have to worry about little things. Your bike and your accommodations should be taken care of. Somebody has to tell you, "Okay, this is what we're going to do. Go shower and then eat a little bit and then we'll have a talk and then you're going to bed."

If you have no support you have to hustle around. Let's say you ride a hundred miles. That's four and a half hours on the bike going pretty hard. Then what are you supposed to do? You'd have to go and get your hotel room while the other teams are being taken care of. Then you would have to spend another two hours cleaning your bike. You'd have to clean your tights, too, and get them ready. All that takes energy, not just physical energy but mental energy.

When you go out and ride a race, you've had it. You don't want to think about anything else for the rest of the day. You want to relax and maybe get a massage and have somebody talking to you building up your confidence for the next day. Even if you don't know that you want it, this is what you need.

Stage races are beloved by many riders because even if you

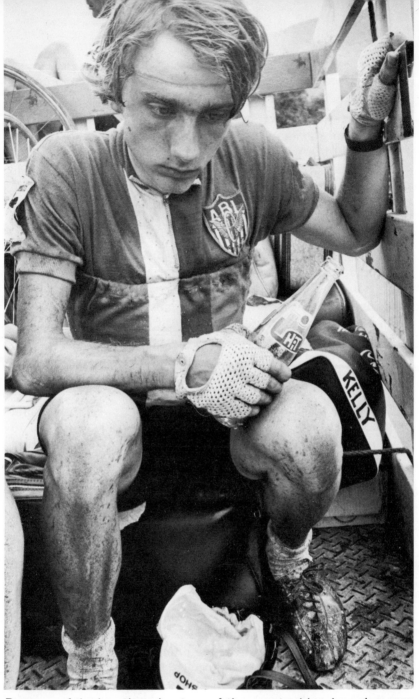

Because of the length and nature of the events, bicycle racing may be the toughest sport in the world.

lose one day, you can still hope to come back and win the next. Because it is so difficult and because it involves several kinds of events, the stage race is felt by many road riders to be the ultimate event in cycling.

CYCLING: THE WORLD'S TOUGHEST SPORT?

In many sports like running or skiing, the athlete who gets to the point of exhaustion has to stop because he can no longer support his own weight. He falls down. In cycling the bike is holding you up and, although this means that you don't need as much energy to support yourself, it also means that all the energy is going into the activity itself. You can suffer much more just doing your thing because you don't have to fight gravity. A rider will sometimes get off the bike after his event and not be able to stand up.

A cyclist can get to the point of exhaustion, where he doesn't have the energy to support his own weight, and still keep on going. He may rest and recover and then reach that point again later on. In many other sports you reach the limit just once.

Cycling events also take longer in terms of hours than most other sports. A marathon runner will race two or three hours one day and then again two or three weeks later and think he's done something. A rider in a stage race has to do two marathons a day every day for a week.

People don't realize how much the human body can do. Believe me, you can do two marathons a day—you are physically capable of doing it—and the world's top professional and amateur cyclists do it practically year 'round.

chapter seven

With the construction of velodromes in new areas of the country and the prospect of building more in the future, increasing numbers of American road riders will be turning to the track for a sharpening of their bike handling skills and the fun and excitement of riding in front of more spectactors.

EQUIPMENT AND CLOTHING

A first and obvious difference between road and track riding is the bicycle. A track bike has a higher bottom bracket to gain more pedal clearance on the banking and thus has a slightly shorter wheelbase. The frame angles are usually 73 to 75 degrees,

track racing

or about the same as a road bike. However, the track bike doesn't have any "gingerbread" on it in the form of brakes, derailleur, bottle cage, etc. It has a fixed-gear direct drive and you can't coast. The average track bike thus weighs between 18 and 20 pounds and feels lighter and more responsive to ride than the road bike. It's like a fighter plane compared to a bomber.

The main difference in track clothing is the fact that the jerseys don't have pockets because, of course, it's not necessary to carry food. Jerseys are often made of silk or a smooth material like helenca or nylon. The silk jersey is a traditional thing; it looks flashier and also cuts through the wind better. A silk jersey does tend to get a lot sweatier than a wool jersey, so it is necessary to change jerseys between races during a meet. Normally

In bicycle racing, the U.S. has had more international success on the track than on the road, thanks to such riders as World Sprint Champion Sue Novara.

you wear a cotton or wool undershirt, which even on a hot day helps take up the sweat better. The undershirt also makes a second layer under the thin-skinned silky jersey and forms a slip if you should crash.

The tights or racing shorts basically are the same except that they would probably be reinforced across the back for team racing. When your partner grabs and throws you in the madison event, it can rip a normal pair of tights right off. Track tights don't have buttons for suspenders or any outside pockets, but they might have an inside pocket for the jamming tool or chucker, also used in team racing.

Shoes and cleats are much the same, although some people go to a half size smaller shoe on the track. This is not quite as comfortable but it's done in sprinting. White socks are optional but are recommended for longer track events because they keep your feet cleaner and you can change them between races. If you don't wear socks you can get dust between your toes and this can be uncomfortable in a hot all-day affair. You generally don't see socks on sprinters or in championship events, but in all-'round track racing and meets promoted for the public you see more socks because the events last longer.

Crank length depends on the event you are riding. For all-'round events, the sprint, and the kilometer, 165 to 167.5-millimeter cranks are usually used. In these types of races the rider has to be all over the track, swinging up and down, accelerating and slowing down quickly, so he wants a real snappy feeling. In the individual pursuit and the team pursuit, the crank length is much more similar to the road, usually 170 millimeters, because you are just riding around the bottom of the track with perhaps one rider swinging up every lap. Pursuiting doesn't involve a lot of maneuvering and jumping and stopping; it's a smooth effort.

Gears vary with the track surface, weather conditions, and particular events, but for general all-'round racing a range of 88 to 90 inches is standard. In sprinting the gear varies between 88 and 94 inches and in pursuiting under very fast conditions it might go up to an occasional 93 or 94.

Tires should be inspected before each ride. This bicycle event is being held on a horse-racing track.

Tires have to be stuck on with a more permanent bond for track racing than for road racing. This is mainly due to the force on the tire when you are going through the turns. Whether you are going through the turns slowly on a steeply banked track or fast on one that's not so steeply banked, there is still a lot of force trying to roll that tire off. The tire is what holds you to the track and if it's not attached with a good hard bond, it could roll off and cause an accident. It should be either shellacked on or put on with 3M rim cement.

Tires should be inspected before each ride to make sure there is nothing coming through; no little nicks or broken treads or anything. You'll find when you get with good riders that they

Good pedal action is one of the most important skills in cycling, as professional World Pursuit Champion Roy Schuiten demonstrates. In the beginning, try to maintain a fairly flat foot position until you find what is natural for you; concentrate on pedaling in a circular motion instead of chopping up and down.

won't tolerate somebody coming to the track with bad tires. If there is training going on and somebody is known to always have bad tires with a lot of patches in them, then he is always forced to ride in the back.

PHYSIQUE AND MENTALITY

A good road rider is built much the same as an all-'round track rider. Pro pursuit champion Roy Schuiten is an example of a good all-'rounder. He was brought up on Dutch amateur racing and rode both the road and the track. He has no trouble adapting to a small six-day track or riding a stage race. He's a well-built man; not heavily muscled and not skinny.

There are all kinds of physical makeups in cycling. You find big heavy guys like Steve Woznick and thin light guys like Roger Young—both of them are Pan American gold medalists. They can both ride criteriums, although Woznick, of course, couldn't ride a road race with mountains because he couldn't get his weight over them.

You don't find too many of the real thin mountain climber types going into track racing. Those mountain riders are kind of special. They are very, very slender and very light-boned and there is really no place for them in track racing.

Riders are closer together in track racing and you have to have sharper reflexes. The smaller the track, the faster you have to think and make decisions. When you're really close in there in the field or in a team race, there are wheels all around you and after a while you develop an instinct to know just where to go. When you come out of a six-day race, for example, your reflexes are so sharp you can actually notice the difference. When you go out on the road everything seems like it's in slow motion.

Track racing definitely does bring out your reflexes compared to road racing where you have a lot of time and long straightaways. Especially in sprinting, if you make the wrong move at the wrong time, the race is over. When you make a decision it has to be the right one or, if it's not the right one, you have to think again very quickly and make another choice. Kilometer riding is a little bit different. There are no real tactical mistakes to be made in a kilometer ride. However, you must be thinking about putting a total effort into the event, even while you're riding. Pursuiting is much the same, but there are subtle tactics involved during the final rounds, when you are racing against an opponent rather than just time.

As far as mentality is concerned, a sprinter can be an impulsive type, someone who has to make a quick decision and stand

Riders are closer together on the track and you must have quick reflexes for events such as this ten-mile scratch race, a National Championship event.

behind it. He commits himself. A pursuiter may be a guy who's going to chase and work on and on and on. It's not something where his effort is done in eleven seconds; he has four minutes to grind it out. So a pursuiter may have a little more even temperament, which may be a little better suited to road racing.

But these are things that can be cultivated, I think. People have all these personality traits in them and they just adapt to the different events. If their temperament is a little more even, they may just lean a little bit more to that type of event. Pursuiters might prefer not to lay themselves on the line for the sprinters' explosion; they prefer to work a little bit.

THE TRACK AND ITS PARTS

A bicycle track or velodrome is an oval riding surface made of

The Dick Lane Velodrome in East Point, Georgia, is a one-fifth mile cigar-shaped track with maximum 34-degree banking. Notice the wide paved flat section at the bottom; this apron can be used as a running track, too.

wood, cement, or macadam, the better ones being either cement or wood. Wood seems to be the fastest surface and cement is reasonably fast, but macadam or blacktop is not that responsive.

There are basically two different shapes of tracks. There is the more oval-shaped or egg-shaped track and then there is the cigar-shaped or long type with short bends. Usually the more oval kind is a little nicer to ride. It's designed, I think, with a little bit more awareness of what the cyclist needs when he's riding and it's easier to pedal around. Of course, you don't just have a track that's one way or the other. There are all different gradients in between.

110

The smaller the track, the steeper the banking needs to be. This portable wood track built in California in 1973 measures 160 meters around and has a maximum banking of 58 degrees.

An oval track is more of a smooth ride because the turn flows into the straightaway. The cigar-shaped track usually has a real dip coming out of the turn and flattens right out in the straightaway and then goes up high into the turn again. All of a sudden, *wham,* you're around the turn making a left-hand turn onto the straightaway. And there it is, this big flat stretch in front of you, and all of a sudden, *crash*, you're into the turn again.

Small tracks can be like that, too. The portable wooden one in California in 1973 was that type. The first couple of times you got on it to ride, *crash*, you're into the banking and then all of a sudden, *whack*, you're thrown back out onto the straightaway and you said, "Where have I been?" But a wooden track the same size that was put up in Detroit that year was the complete opposite. It was so beautiful that you could ride around it blindfolded, standing on your head.

So the egg-shaped, more oval track has a nice flow when you're riding it, but the cigar-shaped track can be a little abrupt going into the turns and coming out and so is a little more dangerous in that respect.

In the center of the track is the infield and around that you have the flat, which is on the bottom of the track and can also be called the apron. It's just a flat part to use when you're mounting the bike or when you're coming off the track.

On good tracks, leading from the flat onto the track itself is a thing called the runners or runner. This is a little curved part, a little dish, so that the slant of the track doesn't make a sharp angle onto the flat and where you can ride up and down smoothly. Although there are nice tracks designed without the runner, it is just a little bit inconvenient to get on and off the track without it.

After the runner, you have the actual surface of the track, the banking. The reason for the banking is for safety, to keep you from slipping when you go around the turn.

On a flat track you are leaning over in the turn at an extremely sharp angle to the surface and your wheel can slip. That's why shallow tracks are not proper racing tracks: they are unsafe. They're just oval bike paths designed for the public to ride around on. They are OK for people on everyday bikes, but they are dangerous for organized racing because, even in a time trial event like the kilometer, it's rough to hold that turn.

These shallow tracks happen because they're built on public land and you're dealing with local politicians who don't realize there's a problem. I believe that the general public can ride on steep banking because in Europe during regular meets they have races for journalists or students and those people don't seem to have any trouble riding right up there first time out.

On really good tracks usually the banking is not symmetrical.

The quarter-mile Meadowhill Park track in Northbrook, Illinois, has a relatively shallow banking of 18 degrees. Starting from the lowest line nearest the infield, the markings are called the pole line, the sprinters' line, and the stayers' line.

The banking going into the turn is a little less steep than the banking coming out of the turn. When you come out onto the straightaway it goes downhill a little bit to the next turn, and so forth. The bike flows around again and it's almost an effortless sensation due to the ever so slight drop on the straightaway. It's nothing that you can see with your eye, but it's felt in the legs.

On a track that symmetrical, as you come into the straight-away there's a slight feeling of going uphill because there's a little hump where the banking starts to flatten out onto the straight. You can feel it because you have to push at that point.

There are several different lines running around the track surface. The most inside one is called the pole line and is where the track is measured. The sprinters' line runs parallel to, and 70 centimeters to the outside of, the pole line. In some races, when a rider comes below the sprinters' line during the final 200 meters of the race, he is considered to have entered the pole and, for safety's sake, must stay below the sprinters' line for the remainder of the race.

The line halfway up the track is called the stayers' line and was put there for motorpacing. It can also be used as a guide for team racing. The riders on relief usually stay above that line.

At the top of the track, hopefully, there is something to keep you from going over the edge, but often there's not. Usually a good track has an overhanging railing that you come up against before you go into the stands or crash into the wall. It should be smooth so you can ride right against it without catching yourself on anything. Usually it's metal tubing. Often there may be just a plywood fence or, on many tracks in this country, just ropes or grass.

YOUR FIRST TIME AT A TRACK

Although there were only twelve tracks in America at the end of 1975, they are widely scattered and riders usually managed to get to them at least a few times a season.

I do not recommend getting on the track with a road bike. It's dangerous because the road bike has a lower bottom bracket and longer cranks. The big danger is hitting the right crank on the banking when you're going slow or, on some tracks in this country, hitting the left crank when you're going around the turn because of insufficient banking.

A road bike with its brakes and freewheel is also not as easy to control as a fixed-gear track bike. To slow down on a road bike, you have to grab the hand brakes, and that takes more time than just relaxing your legs on the pedals as you do on the track bike. By the time you put the brakes on and they grab on the rim, you'd be right into the guy ahead of you. You also lose your maneuverability as soon as you squeeze on the brakes. Relaxing on the pedals of a track bike, however, slows you down quickly and you can even back off a bit, push here, lean there, and you're around somebody.

114

In a warm-up session the train, or fast-moving group of riders, led here by professional and many times National Champion John VandeVelde, snakes around the slower riders. Because this banking is shallow, the slower riders are able to stay near the top, but usually they should be on the bottom and the train should go above them.

There are two places for mounting the track. You can get on from the top by holding on to the railing, waiting until you have a clear space, and then riding down to the bottom. If you get on from the bottom, you have to watch a little bit more closely because it's harder to survey the track from the bottom than from the top. When you see a clear space, have somebody push you off or just roll off yourself and follow the pole line around.

Slow riders should always be at the bottom of the track so that if they should slip down or get a flat, they won't fall in front of anybody. Then the train, the fast-moving bunch of riders, is snaking in and out. They might be riding along the pole line but

115

as they come to slower riders they just snake around them, drop back down in front of them, and keep on going.

In some places in this country, the slow riders are on the top and the fast ones on the bottom. But that's bad because if those riders go to other tracks or to other countries, they would be doing it the wrong way. This confusion probably happens because of the flat banking we have here. On a steeper track it would be harder to stay up high while going at a slower speed, so the slower ones would automatically be on the bottom. But on a shallow track there's no reason for them to be up or down, so they drift all over the place.

If riders are going real slow and talking, they should be off the track and off the bikes. Sometimes at big meets where there are a lot of people on the track, you might see three or four guys riding along just talking. Don't do that. If you're talking to someone you should be off the track, or on the flat.

Get on the track and follow the pole line around. If anybody yells at you, don't get upset or ride erratically or try to get out of the way. Just ride a straight line at all times and usually the other riders will maneuver around. Always be conscious of riding straight, even if you're up high. Don't be in the middle of the track, though, because then riders don't know which side of you to go on.

It's up to you to maneuver around any riders who are in front of you. You could glance to both sides a little bit before passing, because someone could be bearing down on you and you don't want to swing into him. Your movements should be very gradual flowing movements, not quick jerky ones. You can even signal which way you are going to turn. In a pace line, for example, you signal with your elbows. Flick your elbow to the side a little bit and make your turn that way.

Ride along the bottom of the track, rolling comfortably at at least ten miles per hour. Don't get on and feel like you have to start jamming and go as hard as you can go.

After you get accustomed to the feel of what it's like riding on the bottom, go up high and circle around the top a little bit. That's

Anton Tkac of
Czechoslovakia
was carried aloft
by his coach and
teammates when
he won the amateur
World Sprint
Championship.

where you really get the feeling of the banking and the steepness of the track. Ride along the railing fairly hard and get the feel of it, then look for an opening and come back down. Or wait until the pace line comes by and jump in on it for a while.

When a person first gets on a track, even an experienced rider who's been off a steep track for a long time, it feels very, very steep. You feel like you're going to slip off. If you're a brand new rider it might take a few days before you can go up there and feel

117

In the pace line on the track, do not overlap wheels. When pulling off from the front, swing up the banking and let the line go through below you.

relaxed. You'll get the feeling of how slow you can go before you slip down. If you have a proper track bike with a high enough bottom bracket, you will slip off before you hit your pedal, usually. Sometimes when sprinters are practicing, they'll go slower and slower until they feel the back wheel drop a little bit. Before you go so slow that your're going to slip off, usually the wheel will drop once or twice and catch. When you feel that, you know that you've gone slow enough.

If you are riding up fairly high as you go into the turn, it's almost like climbing a hill. You have to push harder to keep your speed up. And then, if you were high up on the banking, as you roll out of the turn it's like going downhill. It might be a funny feeling because you're not used to riding into this wall and being thrown in and out of the turns. But after a little while you adjust to it.

There shouldn't be any echeloning on the track because you don't want to overlap wheels. Everything is closer on the track, though, and you ride about four inches behind the wheel ahead of you. When you swing off the pace line, look first, then swing up to the right.

The biggest mistake riders make is not looking or paying attention. Even when you are walking across the track, you should look to make sure no one is coming. When you make a move, look a little bit, glance around, and don't ride erratically.

The best road men have, many of them, been fine track riders as well. Many American road riders could benefit from time spent on the track. So even if your main interest is on the road, get out to the track to sharpen your skills and reflexes and to increase your speed. Track racing is fast, exciting, and colorful—and well worth your attention for its own sake.

chapter eight

Racing events on the track can be divided into two categories: championship events and mass-start events. Championship events are those ridden at the District and National Championships, the World Championships and Pan American and Olympic Games. They are highly specialized and usually include time trials against the clock; they test the athlete rather than entertain the spectator. Mass-start events are for the all-'round track rider and are more exciting for the spectator: Many riders are on the track at once.

CHAMPIONSHIP EVENTS

The Kilometer, or 1,000-Meter Time Trial

The kilometer is a solo event for amateur men only, ridden from

track events

a standing start over a distance of 1,000 meters (one kilometer). The number of laps ridden, of course, depends on the size of the track, as does the position of the start and finish lines. The rider with the best time wins, there is no second chance, and world class times are below one minute and ten seconds. The difficulty of the event comes in the last half of the ride, when the contestant, riding flat out, has used up the supply of oxygen in his muscles and must continue in spite of great pain in his legs and lungs. Even specialists rarely ride more than a half dozen kilometers in a year.

A kilometer rider, like a sprinter, sits more perched over his bike than an all-'rounder or pursuiter and this is because he has to run on the pedals to get the power, the tremendous explosion, the drive out of his legs. A kilometer bike might be a little stiffer than an all-'round track bike and the gear is usually a 48 x 14, depending on the track. If it's a very fast track, he might go up to a 51 x 15, a 49 x 14, or even a 52 x 15. Although the usual crank length is 165 millimeters, some kilometer riders like to put on a little longer crank, such as 167.5 or 170 millimeters.

Like any other rider, the kilometer man should get on the track about an hour before his event to warm up. He should ride around for about 25 to 30 minutes in a pace line, starting slow and working into a good hard tempo. Then he can change into racing gear and come out and do one good sprint; that seems to help. He still might not have on very light tires and wheels, so just before the event he puts them on and rides around a little bit to make sure everything is right.

I always like to ride through the 1000 meters in slow motion before the race to think about what I'm going to do and how I'm going to feel at the different points. An experienced kilometer rider knows when he's going to want to climb off the bike and when he hits the stone wall; those are the two things that you feel during the ride. So you do one in slow motion and think about it. You could also ride very slowly to where the start is and do a real start for a full lap. Then get off the track and you're ready.

A handler or an official will hold you up for the start. Breathe deeply several times to get as much oxygen as possible. The pedals should be positioned at one or two o'clock. Put some pressure on the pedals before the start so that when the command comes you can get off quickly. You have to start out of the saddle as if you were going to finish in the first turn and when you get there just keep on going.

Usually you have picked out a spot on the track that you know will be a good place to sit down. There's always a tendency to sit down a little bit too early, so when you want to sit down make yourself stay off a little bit. After sitting down, pedal it up to almost a full sprint speed, but hold back from doing that full complete burst, because if you did that you'd just die completely after 300 meters.

Start the kilometer as if you were going to finish in the first turn. National Championship medalist Bob Vehe is out of the saddle and still breathing deeply.

Then you must hold that speed as long as you can. You start to die and you ride right into it and just wear on down like a battery running out of electricity. People have different things they say to themselves at this point to keep going. You can tell yourself something like "Come on, come on." Whatever your individual makeup is, whatever you say normally to yourself to make yourself go faster, that's what you say here.

One mistake people make in the kilometer is trying to save energy in the beginning and not making a good start, or losing time in the start. You have to make that time in the beginning because it can never be gotten back again. No matter what speed you go, you're always going to feel the stone wall. It always comes after a certain time, and if you don't have the speed in the

World Champion Edward Rapp of the Soviet Union fights against pain to maintain his speed over the last meters.

beginning you go into that stone wall slowly and then the party's really over.

Another mistake is to succumb to the feeling, which comes after a certain point, that you're riding a bad kilometer. After about 500 meters you really start to feel tired and you might wonder, "What's wrong with me today?" That attitude can slow you down; you might subconsciously ease up on the pedals a little bit because you're discouraged. But you can't let that happen because it's normal to feel that way. Everybody feels that.

When you go through 500 meters and feel like you want to get off, you really have to fight and grit your teeth to keep going. At 750 meters, when you just can't get those pedals around another time, it flashes through your mind: "I want to stop and do another one. I want to get out of here." You can't even let that thought go through your mind, because it can cost you several hundredths of a second and the race is over. You have to be mentally prepared for these feelings and determined not to let them get the better of you.

The speed of your ride depends upon the weather and the road surface of the track. At Kissena track in New York, if you ride a 1:12 then you're flying. It's equivalent to a 1:09 at Northbrook, Illinois. It also depends on the time of day. At Encino in southern California, there have been some very good times in the early evening after a very hot day when the air is thin and it just quiets down before it gets cool. Those are good conditions. Cool and damp is no good; hot and dry is the best for any kind of times.

An important thing in the kilometer and in any time trial event is to take the shortest line over the distance, or in this case to stay right on the pole line. You cover a lot more ground if you ride high, so it's important for the beginner to concentrate on staying right on the line around the turn. On the straightaways, of course, it doesn't matter too much if you drift up a little bit because you're going the same distance. But in the turns, you might lose five or ten meters if you're not right on the line.

The way to stay on the line, especially on a flat track where it's difficult to hold the turn, is to look 20 yards ahead of you instead of five yards. This will make it easier to follow the track around.

The 1,000-Meter Match Sprint

Although it covers the same distance, the 1000-meter match sprint is very different from the kilometer. Several riders start at once and the winner is the one who crosses the line first, no matter how long it takes. Time is taken on the last 200 meters of the ride, but this time is not used for any judging purposes.

Sprints are a process of elimination and the winner advances through heats to quarter-finals, semi-finals, and so on. Early heats often pit three or even four riders against each other, but the finals are always one against one. There are sprint champion-

Brother and sister Roger and Sheila Young both won National
Sprint Championships in the same year.

126

ships for seniors, juniors, and women on the national and international level.

A sprinter might begin the early season races in a 46 x 14 gear, working up to a 48 x 14 by championship time. Good 200-meter times would be about 12.5 seconds for women and 10.9 to 11.9 for amateur men and professionals.

The tactics of the sprint are based on the fact of wind resistance and the fact that a rider can only go at maximum speed for 200 to 300 yards, after which he starts to fade a little bit. If one rider went flat out from the gun, the other rider could draft right in on him. After 300 yards the lead rider is slowing a little bit, while the man behind is still able to go fast because he's saved all that energy by drafting.

Sprinting involves more than just speed; it takes a lot of thought, too. You have to compute everything. You have to know the track surface and conditions, the wind and where it's coming from, what your opponent is good and bad at, and what you're good and bad at. You make your plans from that.

Sometimes in the first 500 meters nothing happens. The riders set up their positions right away and just go slow and watch one another. But often things do happen. Little things can go on that the spectators or even the other rider or riders in the race don't realize. There's a lot of feinting and faking, where you try to get the other rider where you want him.

I always used to let my opponent do what he wanted to in a race. I had my own thing that I wanted to do, but I'd let him do what he wanted and wouldn't take my position until the very last minute, because it saved a lot of tactics and fooling around. It threw off the opponent. If you let him have the position he wants, then he thinks he has it made. He has confidence and he knows he's going to get you. But when you take it away at the last minute and he has to quickly make another plan, then maybe it's all over.

You can't always get the position you want at the last minute, but it's nice if you can do it. It sometimes requires a lot of maneuvering, jumping underneath and then coming up, holding

The first half of a 1,000-meter sprint match usually involves a lot of jockeying for position. Eventual silver medalist Serge Kravtsov of the Soviet Union is keeping his eye on Junior World Champion Gilbert Hatton of the U.S. while an Italian brings up the rear in this early heat at the senior World Championships.

a rider up high, stalling the sprint a long time, or techniques like that.

If you're a strong sprinter and can ride a good 200-meter time trial, then the front position might be good for you, especially if there is a tailwind on the home straight. A tailwind tends to blow you away. As you come around the turn the tailwind hits the front rider first and so it will push you before it pushes your opponent, making it harder for him to pass.

If there is a headwind on the home straight, then it's nice to pass from the rear. But if you do have to ride from the front, and there's a headwind on the home straight, then stall it as long as possible.

If you are at the front, try to accelerate all the way to the line to prevent your opponents from taking advantage of your slipstream to come by in the final meters.

Any time you are riding from the front you should try to accelerate all the way to the line, which makes it difficult for the rider to pass. You have to gauge your distance to try to keep the sprint short enough to do this.

It's always easier getting the front from the back position than it is getting the back from the front. If you want to take the front you have to do it all at once. Make up a place on the track where you're going to do it. Don't telegraph it to the other rider or show him what you want to do, but just do it quickly.

Generally it's nice to be in the back where you can watch the other rider and don't have to look over your shoulder. There are several ways to maneuver yourself into the rear position and one is by balancing. This is usually allowed after the first lap or the first so many meters and can go on for as long as the contestants wish, provided neither of them goes backwards more than a few inches. If you really want the back, tell yourself that you're going

One way to force your opponent to take the lead is to initiate a balancing, as professional Skip Cutting does here in the World Championships.

to stay there all night and all day if you have to. Be determined.

The way to balance is to face the bike down the track a little bit and turn the front wheel to the right, up the track. That makes a little cradle that rocks you back and forth. The right foot is at about two o'clock and you maintain your position by putting pressure back and forth on the pedals and by moving your left knee in and out for balance.

Sprinters should definitely practice balancing, and not just on the straight because it's simple there. You have to try doing it farther and farther into the turn. You should also practice it just before coming out of the turn, because that's a good place to balance, too. If you fail in your effort going into the turn, drop down to the bottom of the track. Then all of a sudden make a very sharp turn right up before coming onto the back straight, right into the turn, trying to get the other rider to go underneath. If the other rider follows you up, then balance right up there on the steep part of the track, trying to force him to the front.

Some riders seem to be able to ride more slowly through the turn than others. It takes a lot of nerve to go slow when you know you might slip at any time. But if you know from past experience that you've been able to stay up there when others start slipping off, then that's a very good technique for you to use.

Gilbert Hatton shows that the speed you have over the last 50 meters is the most important factor in sprint racing.

Other riders can climb up in the turns. In the middle of the turn, they can go slowly from the bottom of the track up to the top before coming out onto the straight. This can force an opponent to the front. It's usually heavier riders who can do this; they seem to be planted on the track more firmly.

But the most important thing in sprinting is not the tactics but the speed. The speed that you have over the last fifty yards is the most important factor in winning a sprint. It does occasionally happen that a slower man who's a tremendous tactician will beat a faster man. But that's very rare; usually the faster one wins. On a smaller track a tactician may have a slight advantage or a little more of a chance than he would on a larger track.

Where you start your sprint depends on your style and on the other rider and what he's good at doing. If you're a quick snappy sprinter and you're on the front, for example, you don't want to give a really long lead-out; you try and stall it. But if you're a strong sprinter and can get a lot out of a big gear, then you can just go faster and faster and faster. There are sprinters who have won World Championships just by peeling off at about 250 meters and giving a lead-out. They have such good form and top speed that no one can get by. It's like trying to come off an extremely fast motorcycle.

131

Not often seen in the United States, but a crowd-pleasing high-speed event, is the tandem sprint over the 1,500-meter distance. It is part of the World Championships.

Although sprinters only ride fast over the last 200 to 300 meters and go flat out for only about eleven seconds, it is still a very hard event because they have to produce this top speed eight or nine times a day, riding heats, quarter-finals, semi-finals, and so on. It takes a tremendous amount of nerve to keep cool under that kind of pressure. Unlike a kilometer man, the sprinter cannot resolve this pressure with just one ride. He must lay himself on the line again and again, which takes not only tremendous courage but also extreme fitness of its own kind.

132

A very exciting event for spectators is the tandem sprint, one of the fastest events on the track. The team is usually made up of two sprinters, with the bigger of the two usually riding the front position. This makes them more aerodynamic and also more stable. Due mostly to the longer wheelbase bicycle, the moves aren't as quick but when the tandem goes it goes faster. Unfortunately there is not much tandem racing in the United States. It is still part of World Championship competition but has been omitted from the Olympics.

The Pursuit

In an individual pursuit event, two riders start on opposite sides of the track and chase each other for a specified distance. Professionals ride 5,000 meters, amateurs 4,000 meters, and women and juniors 3,000 meters. Times are approximately six minutes, five minutes, and four minutes, respectively.

After the quarter-finals, if one rider catches the other, the race is stopped and he is declared the winner. Otherwise the winner is the one who covers the distance first. The first ride in the series is usually a time trial to determine the top eight or sixteen who will contest in the finals.

The position of a pursuit rider is a little more stretched out than that of a sprinter, with the handlebars slightly higher. He can use lighter equipment because he is pedaling smoothly and not wrenching or twisting the bike like a sprinter or kilometer man. Most pursuiters ride a 15-tooth cog on the back with a 50 or 51 in the front. A 3/32-inch chain is used, the same as on the road, whereas sprinters and kilometer men use a 1/8-inch chain because it's sturdier.

The start should be strong but very smooth. Although you should stay off the saddle about as long as you would in a kilometer ride, you won't be going as fast when you sit down because you'll be riding four kilometers instead of one.

There are tactics involved in pursuiting but not in the first round. For the qualifying ride you and your trainer, if you have

Author Jack Simes gives individual pursuiter Ron Skarin some last-minute instructions on tactics and his schedule during the Pan American Games.

one, decide what time you need to ride to qualify, depending on the track and the wind and so forth. Make a schedule of what your time should be at various distances and he will let you know during the ride if you are up or down on that schedule. If you're a new rider maybe you know that you're not going to qualify, but you just want to ride a good time. At the World Championship level a lot of pursuiters don't use schedules at all. After a while you get to know yourself, you know the distance, and you know just about how fast you can go and still keep going.

The qualifying ride should be a very even ride; you should be finishing almost at the speed you were doing in the middle and maybe a little bit faster if you have something left.

As in an individual pursuit, team pursuiters start on opposite sides of the track and chase each other for the 4,000-meter distance.

In the pursuit, if your energy goes five yards before the line and you feel like you can't go another stroke, that's perfect. I'm sure all experienced bike riders have almost a built-in timer. It comes, learning how to pace yourself.

Another championship event at both the national and international level is the 4,000-meter team pursuit for amateur men. Each team consists of four men who ride in a pace line. Every lap or half lap, the lead man swings up the banking and down onto the end of the line, while the second man pulls through and becomes the new leader. Time is taken on the third man of the team to

The motorpace, or stayer's event, is a fast and exciting race, which uses a special bicycle and a very big gear.

complete the distance, so sometimes the last rider will take an especially strong pull near the finish and drop off after his turn. Because he sits in three quarters of the time, each man can go much faster when at the front of a team pursuit than he would by himself. World-class times for pursuit teams are about twenty seconds faster than individual times. The event favors the fit, fast, and smooth riders who can recover and maneuver quickly. Practice in swinging off **and** pulling through is important so as not to lose valuable seconds.

Motorpace

Though it is not often seen in the United States, the motorpace event is a very exciting one. It is contested between five or ten

(Facing page) The U.S. team of Paul Deem, Roger Young, Ralph Therrio, and Ron Skarin, which took the gold medal at the Pan American Games, had the winning combination of smoothness and speed required in top pursuit teams.

pairs of motorcycle-bicyclists. The bicycle, called a "stayer" bike, has a small front wheel, while the motorcycle has a bar behind its rear wheel that rolls easily if the bicycle should happen to touch it. The motorcycle and driver, who stands up, serve to protect the rider from the wind so he can go much faster (about 50 miles per hour). The driver or pacer's job is very important because he has to keep a steady tempo and ride the best line on the track.

The professional final in the World Championships lasts an hour (amateurs about 40 minutes) and it is a very draining event for the cyclist. It is a different feeling from what is experienced in other events; your whole upper body gets so weak that you can hardly hold yourself up on the bars. This has to do with the high speed that you're traveling, the vibrations, and the time involved. It's a super cardiovascular race. There's not a lot of power used; it's all breathing and blood circulation.

MASS-START EVENTS

In contrast to the championship events, where only one or a few riders are on the track, mass-start events involve many riders. They are usually ridden with a gear of 88 or 90 inches. Sprinters can keep their sprint position but usually it is better to be sitting back more, like an all-'rounder, with the seat a little bit lower and a little bit farther back. A pursuiter could use his pursuit bike because the race never goes so slow that he would hit his pedal, especially if the track isn't steep. The all-'round cyclist is the one who does well in this type of event, and the all-'round position is good—not too low in the front but not quite as high as that of a road position.

The Scratch Race

The simplest of the mass-start events on the track is the scratch race. The contestants all start at the same time, race over a specified distance or number of laps, and the winner is the one who is

Mass-start events are popular in nonchampionship track meets but are also used to determine the national champion among the younger classes of riders, as with these intermediates.

first over the finish line. They are usually short races, but can be up to ten miles long. In fact, a ten-mile scratch race is part of the senior men's U.S. National Track Championships. A crowd-pleaser and held usually at the very end of the program, it is a leftover from the days before specialization and is not ridden in most other countries' championships.

During the race there is attacking, just as in a road race. Riders try to break away and other riders try to chase them down, and there's usually a sprint at the end. You might say that this pattern resembles that of a criterium.

A scratch race is interesting to watch; you see the strengths of different riders coming out. Some are quick and some are strong and they're working on one another. It happens in longer scratch races that a rider or group of riders will lap the field, just as might happen in a criterium on the road. Although it is impossible to get out of sight in a track race, there is a psychological advantage when you gain a half lap on the field.

The number of riders in the scratch race or in most of the other mass-start races depends on the size of the track. On a 400-meter track you could have as many as 30 people riding at once without too much trouble. But on a smaller track you might not want that many. The size of the field also depends on the quality of the riders. If they are inexperienced then you want only ten to fifteen riders; if it's an experienced bunch then you can get away with more. So in general a field can be anything from six to 30 riders.

The Point Race

A point race is a scratch race with a series of sprints and the winner is the man who earns the most points. In this country five miles is a popular distance and the riders might sprint every mile or so. Points can be scored 7-5-3-2-1 or 5-3-2-1 or even 3-2-1 for the top finishers, and sometimes there are double points for the last sprint. An eight-mile point race is one of the events that determines the U.S. Junior Track Champion each year and there is a Junior World Championship point race title also.

If it's ridden aggressively, the point race favors the strong rider, like a pursuiter or a strong kilometer man. Even road riders can do well in this type of event. The sprinters might go out and make a tremendous burst and win the first sprint, but then everybody attacks and it's all over for them. The pattern is for everyone to sprint, then right after the sprint there's an attack, and then another sprint, and some more attacks on top of that. Pretty soon it's broken wide open. It's a good event for endurance riders.

The most important thing in a point race is to be consistent. You can win the event without ever winning a sprint, just by going on the right wheels and making the right move at the right time. Sometimes, for example, it doesn't pay to try to move from third to first when you're on the home straight if you have to put out a tremendous effort just to do that. It's better to take a few points and be ready for the next attack or the next sprint. If an attack is going that looks like it might stay away, you want to be able to go with it.

In the point race you have to keep in mind how many points you have. You have to do a little calculating because you want to save as much energy as possible. You also have to realize how many points everybody else has. You do this almost automatically by knowing who's around you in the sprint. If you're in contention and got third in a particular sprint, keep in mind who got first and second; these are the ones you're going to try to beat the most.

Try to place high, to get into the top three; when you're doing this, if one of the riders who beat you in the first sprint is ahead of you, then he's the one you have to watch. If you're ahead of him, then you just keep trying to place consistently. You don't have the whole field to worry about—usually it's just the better riders. Of course, you do lose track sometimes. Many times at the end nobody knows who won the thing until they add up all the points.

The Miss-and-Out

In the miss-and-out race, the last person over the line on each lap or every other lap is removed from the race. It's an elimination contest and is run down to the last two or three riders, when it becomes something like a match sprint. The finish is not as much cat-and-mouse as a match sprint because the riders are a little bit tired by then. They go slow and watch each other but there's none of the usual jockeying and balancing.

A miss-and-out race is not just a few good sprinters or a few strong men in the front trying to accelerate. It's not the winner across the line who's getting points in the race. It's the last one who's got to watch out, so the fellows in the back keep trying to rush past. Every time they come to the line it makes the field accelerate very fast, because everybody's trying to make sure he doesn't get out. That really keeps it moving.

This is a good event to ride from third or fourth position; one thing that's very important is not to get caught underneath other riders. Never get overlapped on the inside of a wheel. Always stay to the outside of the rider in front of you so that when the rest of the riders come with the field there's room for you to pass.

If you're on the inside you can't go to the front: the lead rider is on the pole and the other ones are stacked up a little behind him, because they're all looking for clearance to go through. The riders behind will come by very closely and close you in on purpose. If a rider has a chance to box in another rider in a miss-and-out he'll do it, almost 100% certain, because that enables him to coast to the line without accelerating too much. He can see that you can't get through if you're underneath, on the inside.

If you're a new rider coming into one of these mass-start races on the track, especially the miss-and-out, you shouldn't try to make holes. Don't try to bump and push your way through. If you've gotten into a bad position and you're going to be called out, go out. It's better than making a crash.

Team tactics can be used in a miss-and-out race. One very strong rider in the front makes a steady tempo all around the track, which strings the other riders out. When he gets onto the home straight he starts to ease up just a little bit, and as he eases up everybody's trying to move fast. If there are enough riders, this stacks them up right across the track and then those in back can't get through.

After they cross the line, the strong man starts rolling again, faster and faster, three-quarters of the way around the track. As he comes out into the home straight again, he eases up just a little bit and that stacks them up again. The riders who are in second or third position—his teammates usually—have it really nice just sitting there.

The Handicap

The handicap is a very good race to watch, and it's valuable

142

In the handicap event on the track, the limit rider, at left, has the shortest distance to travel and the scratch men, at right, the longest. Lines had not yet been painted on this 333 1/3-meter 27-degree track in Trexlertown, Pennsylvania, in time for the opening meet.

training, too. It's useful preparation for all types of events. That's why the Australians are such good track riders; they have handicaps, handicaps, handicaps. The race can be any distance from a quarter mile up to several miles, but the better ones are very, very short. The limit riders, who have the shortest distance to travel, are spaced about ten yards apart; closer to scratch there may be five yards between each man.

The handicapping is usually done by the race director; if it's done right, all the riders come together right towards the end in a string and everybody's trying to pass. It's very spectacular.

A handicap rider has a push to get him started; as soon as the gun goes off, the pusher runs with the rider. He holds his left hand on the top tube and his right hand under the saddle, and he runs; he lets go with his left hand and gives a real hard shove with his right. Just before he lets go he yells "up" to the rider, who then gets out of the saddle.

143

If you are on or near scratch you're trying to catch the rider in front of you, and that rider is trying to catch the man in front of him, so it's really moving. Even when there are only five yards between you and the man in front, he's starting as fast as you are so if you don't have a good pusher and a good start, you might have trouble catching. Scratch is a nice place to be once you catch the man ahead of you, because you can see what's happening in front. If you're two spaces up, though, and you don't catch right away, you can end up doing work for the scratch man, and that's not too good. If he gets on you right away and you can't catch your man, then you're going to be cooked at the end.

Usually just as everyone comes together it'll be going into the sprint, so there's not much sitting on; you have to move really quickly. Just go as hard as you can and get on that wheel ahead; you might even start to pass immediately.

Team Racing, or The Madison

Team racing on the track is a very complex type of event, and you might not ride one in your first year. But once a rider gets involved in track racing that's usually what he wants to do most of all, because it's the most fun. It's also one of the most exciting races to watch.

A team race consists usually of five or ten teams of two or three men. Each team has its own color jersey so the other riders will know who the team members are. Distances are twenty miles or more. The event should last at least a half hour; a one-hour race is very nice. The riders on the team take turns in the race, relaying each other in by a handsling or a throw from the seat of the pants. Because two or more riders are taking turns, the average speed is high, about 30 to 35 miles per hour.

While the team race is going on it consists of three groups of riders. There's the field, which is made up of the riders contesting the race at that time. On the very bottom of the track are the riders who have just thrown their partners in and are going on relief. On the top of the track are the ones waiting or just about to

144

come off relief. The field snakes through those two latter groups.

As you come to your partner, he drifts down off the top of the track. You grab him by the jamming tool or chucker, which is attached to his tights at the upper left hip. You throw him in and he fits right into the slot you just left. Pushing him in automatically slows you down and the field passes on the outside. As you're going into relief, you have to watch all the time to make sure everybody has passed you. When they're all past, you go up to the top of the track and become one of the ones who are waiting to go off relief.

When a team or several teams are attacking, trying to get away or to gain a lap, it can be very confusing to the new spectator. He or she can sit there exclaiming, "I don't understand this. What's going on?" But after a little while it becomes apparent what's happening, especially if there's someone there to explain it or if it's written in the program how it works. Once you've learned how to watch it, it can be very exciting.

A team race can have one finish at the end and it can have different sprints for points. The way it usually works is to first score on the distance. If there's a team one or two laps ahead of the other teams, then they're the winners. But if you have several teams on the same lap or even all of them, then it's scored by the points that have been accumulated in the various sprints or by the placing in the finish if there's only one sprint.

Attacking in team racing is usually done from the first few places. It can be dangerous to attack from farther back, because there's a tremendous amount of traffic to weave your way through. Riders are coming in and others are going off, and usually by the time you make your way through them and get clear you've probably come to your own partner and have to throw him in. Any stacking up of riders is dangerous; a team race is usually just a line of riders.

To attack, you have to maneuver yourself into the proper position close to the front. Sometimes it's good to attack just as your main opponents are making a change, especially if it's quite close to the end or close to a sprint.

The relay method used by amateurs in team racing is to push the partner into the race by means of the jamming tool in his left rear pocket.

One way to attack is by going up the banking. For instance, as you're coming into the straightaway, instead of following the field around, ride right up to the railing instead. 'If you go very hard along the railing, usually there's nobody sitting right on you, and so you draw even with the leader coming into the turn. Use the banking to swish down ahead of him, and you're on your way. You've gotten that extra speed off the banking and can get a few yards that way.

As in other mass-start events, beginners should remember never to pass underneath. For instance, when there's a team making a relief right in front of you, you should never go underneath that team. Always go to the outside of it.

In changing partners, the man who is coming in has to watch for his teammate and get in a position to be picked up. The one

146

The handsling is often used by professionals in team racing.

who is coming on relief will be riding on the pole and the other one must drop down to the sprinters' line. As the first man comes through underneath, he'll grab the new rider and push him in.

The proper way to push is to grab the jamming tool on the left-hand side of your partner's tights. If you're moving quite fast your hand will probably go all the way to the back of you as you pass him. The push is two motions. You pull him up to your side and then you push with your shoulder, almost as if you were pushing him across your front wheel.

Another thing to remember is where to hold your left hand. When you're about to push your partner in, hold the bars on the top with the left hand. Grasp the bars across the extension with the index finger and thumb. Don't hold the bars just with a fist. The index finger across the stem stabilizes you.

You should definitely change partners every time you come abreast of your teammate. You have to do this because the race is going so fast that you get tired in one lap. A team race is really like a series of interval sprints. After you've done one, you're not ready to do another one on top of that. Often if one rider misses a pickup his team loses the race right there. It's very important never to miss.

The only time when one rider might take a longer turn and purposely skip a pickup is toward the end of the race. There might be one strong rider who can go an extra lap in order to set up the other partner for the sprint.

OTHER EVENTS

There are many other track events. One that has almost vanished from the scene is the Australian pursuit. Instead of two riders on the track, there are five or six, depending on the size of the track, and they're spaced evenly around. When a rider is caught by another rider, he is eliminated from the race, which continues until there is only one man left.

The Italian pursuit, on the other hand, is a form of team pursuit, with two teams of four to six riders. Each lead rider of a team pulls one lap, and when he crosses the line he swings up and leaves the race. At the end only one man is left from each team.

There's also an interesting consolation race that is run occasionally after a sprint series or handicaps. It consists of three places and three sprints, perhaps every other lap. The rider who wins the first sprint wins the race and he drops out. Then they go another lap or two and the one who wins the second sprint gets second and he's out. Then everybody dashes it out for third.

WINNING QUALITIES

A short scratch race is often a sprinter's race but a longer event, like a ten-mile, can be anybody's race. A strong sprinter can win, or a pursuiter who can bust everybody up and get rid of the weaker riders by attacking and maybe even gaining a lap by himself or with some others. It depends on the length of the race.

A point race is similar. Everybody's in there—the sprinters, pursuiters, and road types—and the winner might be a rider who's fairly fast but can attack time and time again. He can go with anything that goes and he has a good sprint, too. All-'round riders do well in point races. If you go hard and place as high as possible in each sprint, making sure to be consistent, they you're going to be in the money.

In a miss-and-out, the winner usually has a good sprint and can repeat it often. He has to be a good bike handler and not afraid to rough it up, either. A sprinter will usually fare a little better in a miss-and-out than he will in a point race.

A handicap race is designed so that everyone is more or less on equal terms with 400 meters to go. The sprinters start at scratch and the pursuiters would be placed farther up. If it's designed properly, the sprinters might be able to just squeak by. But a good strong rider who doesn't have too much speed might make it, especially if the crowd is rooting for him to go and beat the other guys. Longer handicaps begin to benefit the pursuiter.

A team race rider has to have all these qualities plus a special amount of agility and quick reflexes, because there are so many people on the track. The race is a lot longer, so he also has to have more endurance. But he also has to be really fast, to close gaps and sprint well. He has to be able to repeat. Recuperation is a big factor here because he has only about 30 seconds' rest before his partner comes around again to pick him up. Then he has to do it again, and that can go on for an hour. The team race is considered by many to be the ultimate challenge and the most satisfying event in track racing.

No matter what the event on the track, however, the same riders usually win consistently. Sometimes there's a winner who's a fluke, but usually riders who win or place in the top three or five are the ones who do it all the time. They are the ones who were born with the right genetic combination and the ones who have worked the hardest to develop their talents. This is the winning combination.

chapter nine

WHAT TO DO IN WINTER

When the racing season is over in your area—perhaps in October or November—you are faced with the question of what to do in the winter. If you plan to race the following season, you should not just hang up the bike and get fat. Your next season will be much easier if you maintain a certain level of fitness. If you quit completely you will have to start building all over again in the new year and might waste several months that could have been more productively spent.

Over the winter you want to maintain your oxygen uptake, keep fat off your body, and keep your muscles conditioned. It is good for you to relax from competition, and a week or two of doing nothing won't hurt you. But for most of the off season

training

you should keep active, either riding your bike regularly if that's possible, or engaging in some other form of exercise such as skiing, running, hiking, skating, weight lifting, or even just calisthenics.

Europeans are lucky enough to have an indoor track season during the winter, but there are several other ways to stay in the saddle all year round. Cyclocross racing can be done in bad weather conditions and over rough courses, while roller racing or training can be done indoors. Both of these provide variety and exercise, yet still keep the legs moving and the rear end in condition.

Cyclocross

Cyclocross is an activity used by many Europeans to keep in

151

The sport of cyclocross provides valuable training in bike handling because of the difficult courses and tricky surface conditions.

With its combination of running and riding, cyclocross is a tough endurance activity.

shape during the off season, but is also a full-fledged sport in its own right. There are National Championships and World Championships each year. Cyclocross events are popular with spectators because they are exciting and easy to watch.

The cyclocross season starts in late fall and culminates in the World Championships in January or February. Events are held on one- or two-mile circuits over a distance of ten to 15 miles and last up to an hour. Courses include running and riding both uphill and downhill over mud, grass, pavement, and even stairs.

Although there are obstacles or difficult sections that force the rider to dismount—creek beds, logs, and so on—cyclocross is still bicycle racing and less than a quarter of the race is customarily spent on foot. Running stretches rarely last long and there is often a choice of whether to ride or run. The start and finish are usually on a straight and paved section of the course, so even a sprint is sometimes necessary.

Cyclocross races have been won on all types of equipment, but

152

there are some things it is nice to have. Cyclocross tires have better traction; tire pressure should be lower than that used on the road for the same reason. Wheels last longer if built with heavier rims, and both frame and brakes should have greater wheel clearance to allow for mud buildup. A high bottom bracket and shorter cranks also help road clearance.

Pedals should be wide; double toe-clips provide extra durability. The saddle clamp should be very securely fastened because of the constant stress of mounting and dismounting. Chain guards are useful and handlebar shifters provide better control. Shoes are especially important and soccer-style heel cleats help in running, while extra-long laces tied around the back keep the shoe from coming off in the mud.

When riders have to get on and off their bikes as many as 100 times in a race, it is obvious that efficient mounting and dismounting can save valuable minutes. Dismount on the left by pulling the left cleat slightly out of the pedal. Coast to running speed while swinging the right leg over the saddle and putting it forward between the left leg and the bike; meanwhile, grab the down tube with the right hand. Stride forward on the right foot at the same time as you slip the left foot out of the pedal and shoulder the bike.

Remount the bike at a run by setting it down and holding the bars in both hands. Leap into the saddle and insert both feet in the toe-clip at once. This is not easy to do, and top Europeans spend many hours in the early season just slipping their feet in and out of both pedals at once. Mounting and dismounting should be practiced to make them smooth, safe, and quick.

When riding difficult sections, keep your weight back on the saddle over the rear wheel for best traction both up and down hill. For stability, pedal on descents as much as possible; keep the weight on the outside pedal over the tires on the turns.

Small light endurance athletes do best in cyclocross, but a great amount of skill in bike handling is also necessary to navigate the difficult courses at top speed. Many riders who take up cyclocross just for fun find unexpected benefits in skill and confidence under bad road conditions during the regular racing season.

Bicycle Rollers

Rollers are used by most cyclists at various times and in various ways. At the track, or before a road race where space is limited, they are used to warm up for events. People train on rollers when the weather is bad or if there's not enough time to go out on the road. I sometimes use them to loosen up after a short cold outdoor session. Groups of rollers can be linked with dials for competition.

Either a road or a track bike can be used, but be sure to adjust the rollers to the wheelbase of your machine. The back wheel centers itself naturally between the two back rollers and the front axle should be directly above the axle of the front roller. If the front wheel is positioned too far back, the bike will wobble; if it is too far forward, you might ride right off the front when accelerating.

I like to wear full-length warm-up pants and a long-sleeved jersey when I ride the rollers. Place the rollers in a door frame or near a wall so that you can support yourself if necessary; you can use a chair for mounting. Ride in the usual training position with the hands on the top of the bars, not down on the hooks. You'll be able to breathe better and stay smoother on the bike.

Tires should be inflated a little more than would be normal for the road. Soft tires make the ride bouncy and mushy. Gearing for a road bike should be 52 x 14 or 53 x 14. On a track bike, use 49 or 50 x 14. Staying upright is just a matter of balance, and you will soon learn to ride no-hands. When beginning, remember not to hold on too tight and don't panic. Falling doesn't really hurt when you're not going anywhere.

In cold weather, if you want to train seriously but can only get outdoors for short rides, it's good to use rollers during another part of the day. If you ride the road in the evening, for example, then use rollers in the morning. Spending half an hour or an hour on the rollers after coming in from a ride can help fitness.

Bicycle rollers can be used for home training or to warm up for events, as Sheila Young does here. During the winter there are often roller competitions.

If there's a long stretch of time when you can't get out on your bike, perhaps four days or more, then you should get on rollers every day. Do a hard interval workout for an hour one day and a shorter, easier ride at moderate tempo for about half an hour on alternate days.

For a good one hour workout, start with a slow tempo and ride ten or 15 minutes until you are just starting to sweat. Then do 15 or 20 minutes of fast tempo, with the last five minutes extra fast. When you finish, you should be so exhausted that you can't go another 30 seconds at that pace. Roll slowly again for five minutes to rest. Then do 15 interval sprints, 30 seconds on and 30 seconds off. Spend another five minutes at slow tempo to finish the hour.

You should be quite tired at the end of this workout. If you are still getting in shape or don't have an hour to spend, cut down the number of minutes spent on each activity to make perhaps a 45-minute training session.

Roller racing is done with a track bike and the competition distance is usually one mile. The maximum gear allowed is 50 x 14 and maximum wheel size is 27 inches, with a minimum crank length of 165 millimeters. Tilt the hooks forward and upward to provide a more level surface on the top of the handlebars. Position yourself directly over the pedals for better spin by dropping the saddle and moving it forward. Be sure to have the ball of the foot directly over the axle of the pedal; this is a farther-back foot position than some road riders are used to.

More speed work is necessary if you plan to race on the rollers. The standard one-hour workout can be alternated with a more specialized routine. Begin with the warmup, then do five interval sprints of 15 seconds each with 30 seconds' rest between each one. Roll ten minutes then do a mile (about one minute) flat out; roll another ten minutes and do another one-mile sprint. If you're feeling all right, do this a third time as well, then end with ten minutes at a moderate tempo.

Keep Riding

In warm weather climates, all a rider has to do to stay in shape is to give himself a little schedule of various types of rides that he's going to take in the winter—nothing strenuous because there's no reason for it at that time of year. If you're not racing for four or five months, 50 to 65 miles is plenty of riding each day. The schedule may vary by going for a 50-mile ride three times a week and on the other days going 35 miles.

People in cold climates should also follow a schedule like that if they can, if the weather isn't bad. Cold weather can be really annoying, but you should make yourself go out every day no matter what the temperature is, unless it gets down to ten or fifteen degrees, when it's hard to go out for a decent ride. What people do in extremely cold climates in order to get their training is to go out for about ten miles on a local circuit. They come back in and warm up and then go back out again. That is very time-consuming, so they can't get as fit as early as other riders.

Don't overdress for a training ride, but wear enough clothes so that when you first start out you're not freezing. You're going to warm up when riding anyway, but you should have enough on to keep the wind out and keep the cold away from your body. No matter how cold it is you always start to sweat a little bit. Parts of your body, such as feet and hands, may be frozen, but you can still be sweating.

156

Keep riding through the winter if you can and be sure to dress warmly, as these riders did for an early season training race in New York's Central Park.

Even later on in the season, as long as it's not brutally hot out, it's always good to wear a long-sleeved jersey and long tights. Some riders make a point of training with warm and even loose-fitting clothing on. They sweat more and the outfit grabs more wind, so they have to work harder. Then when they get in a race they feel good, which helps their morale. If you can put up with it, anything that makes your body work under a little bit more stress is a good idea.

Spring Training

If you're fairly fit from the winter but haven't been racing, then a month to six weeks before the start of the season you should begin your preparation. This is no different from the riding you were doing over the winter, but you must increase the distance and the gears. If you were taking 35-mile rides at a medium tempo, then you might go on a 50-mile ride at the same tempo. Or do the 35-mile ride at a faster tempo. By increasing the tempo a little bit here and there, and increasing the gear in the same way, you build up your training as the season goes on.

The Weekly Schedule

The weekly training schedule for a nationally ranked rider might go something like this:

Monday, after a Sunday race, a 50- to 65-mile ride in a fairly small gear of about 75 inches over fairly flat terrain.

Tuesday, a very rapid tempo ride of about an hour and a half in that same gear, very fast. You might warm up for 15 minutes and then just twiddle along, breathing and sweating for about half an hour, take a five-minute break, do another half hour, and then roll down easily for fifteen minutes.

Wednesday, another long ride. If you are fairly far along into the season, you might do over 100 miles, mostly in a small gear. If you had some nice stretches of road or were feeling good, you'd start going up into your racing gears (53 x 13, 14, 15, 16, etc.) for half an hour or so, just to get the feel of it.

Thursday, repeat what you did Tuesday.

Friday, 80 miles or so, not too hard. If you feel good, then step into it a little bit.

Saturday, before Sunday's race, an easy 40 miles just riding around.

Earlier in the season or for juniors and women these distances can be halved, then gradually increased, depending upon the individual and category of his or her racing. The 100-mile ride might only be 60 miles, and Monday's 60 miles might be only 30. The tempo ride on Tuesday you probably wouldn't even do at all; you'd probably just go out and ride around.

If you're racing both Saturday and Sunday, your Friday ride would be a little easier. The best riders get on the bike every day; there's no off-day. But the day before a race you don't want to be knocking your brains out; that's why you do about 40 or 50 miles of nice riding, with a little bit of brisk effort in there just to feel good.

The only reason to spend any real leisure days is if your legs are tremendously heavy. Perhaps over the weekend you've ridden some super-hard races with great big gears and you're tired and disgusted. Then you might even take Monday off, and do 50 miles of easy riding on Tuesday.

When there are short club races or training races during the week, in the evening you should still get out in the morning and do some riding. Put in 35 to 40 miles of brisk pace in a small gear, about 75 inches. The little gear won't hurt you; it makes you breathe and work hard, but you recuperate. You recover immediately and it doesn't bother your legs.

The alternation of slow and fast and short and long days gives you different types of training. Long slow days work on leg muscles and take fat off the body. Short fast days are for the cardiovascular system and breathing. Both types of fitness are necessary for road racing. You have to be able to make a quick hard short attack, to sprint a little bit and be able to bridge gaps. But you have to be able to finish the race; your legs have to be in good shape at the end of the race, too.

A technique that is good for your cardiovascular system is interval training, which can be done during part of the ride. Intervals are used in training for many sports and can be described as a series of sprints that build up strength, tax the system, and teach recovery. You don't put out absolute maximum effort for each sprint because you'd be finished after two or three times. You use about three-quarter effort. The length of the sprint can be determined by time or by leg revolutions or by distance, and different people prefer different length intervals. I find that in cycling a good interval to choose is about 400 yards, or perhaps the length of four telephone poles along the side of the road. A series of five or ten of these with equal amounts of rest in between can help build heart and lungs, endurance, and speed.

What Time of Day to Train

Ideally training should be done in the morning. Get up at 7:30, have breakfast at 8:00, and then go out on your ride an hour later at about 9:00. You can take another ride in the evening about 4:30. This is the ideal situation, of course, but people can't do that; they have to work. When I have things to do during the day, then I go out at 7:00 in the morning.

The morning seems to be a good time to train because, although by 9 o'clock it's warming up a little bit, the air is still fresh out and nice. It seems cleaner. By the end of the day it can get hot and there are a lot of auto fumes around. There is less wind in the morning, too; the wind seems to come up and go down with the sun.

Midday doesn't seem to be a good time to train, especially in the summer when it's hot. Also it's getting around lunchtime and you've either just eaten or you're getting hungry.

Evenings are nice for training, especially on the track. But often you can't pick and choose the ideal training time, and must make the best of your own situation. So be flexible.

Specialization and Individual Needs

Training is a building process. You start out with shorter rides and the tempo builds, the gears build and the mileage builds. All riders start out with basically the same training program, but part way through the season they begin to specialize. The road rider keeps on increasing his gears and his mileage (or, if he's doing a lot of hard racing, he's taking it easy between races), while the track rider, especially the sprinter, starts to cut down on his miles. He goes shorter road distances because when he climbs on his bike at the track his legs have got to be absolutely fresh.

The time to start specializing is dictated by the time when the specialty races are due to start. If they are important ones the rider might start six or seven weeks before. But if it's just weekly racing on the track, the first time he goes out to the velodrome for a workout might be just the week before.

In Europe and in some parts of the United States riders are lucky enough to have almost daily racing during the season, so they don't have to worry about training. There's not much need for training when they can use the races to train. If they feel good then they'll go with some breaks and try to win, or they might not go to win but just sit in the field. This is one reason Europeans don't have a very rigid attitude about training. They get all the different kinds of training in their racing; they get interval sprints and they get the long slow distances and everything

160

combined into one. If they don't feel like doing it, they just drop out.

The amount of training to do seems to depend on the toughness of the individual's character and physique. You could take two different people and put them on the same training program. One person goes out and does it and feels terrific, and he wants more. But the other can't go out and do it again or perform properly the next day. Perhaps he needs a little different schedule; he should cut down while the other man should do a little bit more.

Improvement is a long slow process and it's not a thing you can feel. When you first start training two weeks will go by and you don't even feel as fresh as when you started. It actually feels like you're down a little bit. But keep on doing it. It'll take four or five or six or seven weeks before you'll be able to go out there and feel like you can conquer the world.

After the weeks go by you're going better. You don't even realize it until all of a sudden one day you've made a tremendous ride in a big gear, which you couldn't have done a few weeks before and you still feel light on the pedals. Or on the track you're sprinting for three or four weeks and all of a sudden you don't even realize it but you're going faster.

The important thing is to get out and do something; not something that's making you exhausted every day, but something you can do again and again and again. Whether you're the kind of person who has to sit down and make up schedules and follow them or the kind of guy who likes to go out for long rides and just tempo away mile after mile, what's important is spending time on the bike.

When the races start coming along they're going to fill in the gaps that you've left in your own training. If you're not somebody who can sit down and see where your weaknesses are and work on them, the racing after a few weeks is going to fill in these gaps. Racing is an important part of training because you get all kinds of riding there, whether you like it or not.

chapter ten

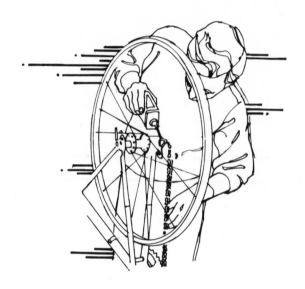

BIKE MAINTENANCE

In order to win the race you have to get to the finish line, and so you are dependent on your equipment. If you are a professional, for example, and are paid money to compete, then your equipment has to be 100% perfect. If you have faulty equipment, the sponsor is not going to give you another contract. It's as simple as that; your equipment cannot let you down at all.

Cleaning and Lubrication

When training regularly on the road, it is best to clean the bike every few days. Don't let it get bogged down with dirt, because it

maintenance
and health

won't work as well. Cleaning is also a good time to lubricate and check the bike over for frayed cables, looseness, and so on.

Every couple of days I hose down my bike. I put degreaser all over it and then take a garden hose and spray it off, dry it, and lubricate the moving parts.

De-greaser or "gunk" is also used on motorcycles. It's a compound that penetrates grease and turns into a soapy foam when water hits it. Put the de-greaser all over; on the chain, on the derailleur, on everything. Wrap up the bottom bracket with little strips of cloth so the water won't get in, then hose the whole thing down. It will take everything off—all the dirt and all the grease.

Dry the bike including wheels, rims, and spokes, and lubricate

163

A thorough cleaning every few days keeps the bike in good working order and provides a chance to check the various parts for wear.

everything properly right away. There are some special spray lubricants made just for the chain. The thick one that I use is called LPS#3. It's a lubricant that doesn't pick up dirt like oil would; it's probably got some silicone in it. I spray that on the chain and wipe it off immediately. Then there's no chance of any rusting.

With a pump-type oil can, I put a little drop of oil in all the bearing points. Every part with bearings or friction points has to be lubricated. Normally there are bushings in the derailleur instead of bearings and these must be lubricated also. I spray lubricant down in the cables and wherever there's a pivot point on the brakes. Everything that moves should be lubricated slightly and then wiped off so that it doesn't pick up dirt. Finally I pump some oil in the hubs and lay the bike over to let the excess drain out, and the bike is ready to go.

This whole cleaning process might take half an hour, but it's

Lubricate the chain and all the bearing points with a pump-type oil can.

worth it. Some people take the whole bike apart to clean it. I used to do that but it takes too long. You may be reluctant to spray your bike with water, but as long as you don't let any get inside, and you oil and dry it right away, there's no problem at all.

When training in a lot of rain or dirt, it's not a bad idea to tie little strips of cloth on your bike before a ride. Wrap them around the bottom bracket where the cranks go into the spindle. You can also wrap strips of cloth around the hubs, right around the cone nuts. Another place is around the bottom part of the head bearings. This keeps the dirt and water from getting into these places when you ride. It is a pain in the neck to take apart something like the bottom bracket, so if you protect it you'll save yourself a lot of time.

The Check-Up

Every time you clean the bike, or periodically, there are certain things to watch out for, such as the head bearings and bottom bracket bearings. Bearings should always be kept in proper adjustment, not only because it makes riding easier and more efficient but because it reduces wear.

If you have the wheel off, hold the axle in your hands and spin the wheel slowly. It should turn freely with no hesitation or gritty feeling.

When the wheel is in the frame, put your hand on the rim up by where it passes through the fork and try to move it from side to side. There should be no play or motion in there. If the cones are loose, there's going to be movement from side to side. There shouldn't be any play in there at all. There should be just the tiniest little crack of feeling. If you feel something but the wheel doesn't move from side to side, then that's the proper adjustment.

As the brake pads wear down, the brake handles pull farther into the bar. It's not safe to have them pulling so far in that they almost touch the bar and barely stop. Most brakes have an adjustment that you turn, but occasionally you may be all the way to the end of the adjustment and have to pull some more cable through.

When the brake blocks get worn down to a certain point they have to be replaced. If you have to adjust the brake so that it's pinching too much and putting a lot of tension on the spring, then it's time to replace the pads. You should be able to get half a season out of a set of brake blocks.

A very important thing, especially for track riders, is to check the tires. First of all, they must be glued on properly. Then spin the wheel very slowly to see if there are any small cuts that go through the rubber tread onto the cord. A blowout, especially on the track, not only means that you crash but probably that others come over you.

The beginning of the season is the time to take everything apart, just strip the frame down. While the bike is apart, it's always nice to paint it, to start off the fresh season with a fresh bike. It gives you a better outlook. Some riders even like to start the season with an entirely new bike, if they can afford it.

When you take it apart, clean everything out and check for wear. If the bearings look worn or cracked, if the cups look worn in the bottom bracket, then you replace these.

If the chain has been on for a long time, it will get worn, and this makes it a little bit sloppy sideways sometimes. There are problems using a worn cluster with a new chain or vice versa; the chain will jump. So every time you replace a cluster you should replace the chain. If you keep the chain clean you can get at least one season out of it. It's nice to have two chains—one for racing and one for training, just like the wheels.

Perhaps every two months you should clean the bottom bracket. If you're riding in a lot of rain it has to be cleaned every couple of weeks to get the dirty grease out. If you're riding on a road where there's a lot of dirt, sand, and grit, then you also have to pull the bottom bracket apart and clean it. At that time check to see if the cups are pitted. If they look smooth, then everything goes back in, but clean. Make sure the bearings are packed in plenty of grease. When you put the bottom bracket back in, make sure it's in adjustment the same way the hubs are in adjustment. There shouldn't be any play but you should feel a little bit of something when you move it back and forth. It should roll easily.

Cables have to be lubricated a little bit but you should get at least a season out of them. If the hubs are kept in proper adjustment they should last practically as long as you're racing.

A bike that runs smoothly and looks nice presents a good image and helps upgrade the sport. Don't ride a bike that is all muddy and dirty. Even the handlebar tape should be kept clean. It gives you good morale to have a nice clean-looking bike under you.

Should You Do Your Own Work?

I don't think it's important to do your own work on the bike unless you don't have the money to hire anyone or if, when you get to a big race, there aren't any competent team-supplied mechanics around. Don't give your bike to just anybody to work on; make sure the mechanic is race-oriented and of good reputation. Otherwise do it yourself to make sure that it gets done properly. From time to time I have lost races because I've let other people work on my bike. Once in a World Championship I lent my bike to another rider and he forgot to change the gear before giving it back to me. So I was out there with a training gear on. Things like that can happen.

Once you get on an Olympic team or become a professional, there are mechanics who can do the work much better than you can because they are professionals, too, in what they do. You give the bike to them and you don't have any headaches to worry about. You can spend your time doing something else.

Very few clubs in this country have paid mechanics, so I think most riders here do their own work. Some riders' fathers like to work on bikes and they are just as meticulous as any mechanic so they do a good job.

It's a good idea if you have the money and there's a good racing shop nearby, to have them do the work. I know one rider who took his bike to a shop every time he rode in the rain, because it was too much trouble for him to clean it. He'd pay $15 to have it cleaned and oiled, which isn't bad. If you figure what your time is worth and that it might take a couple of hours to clean and oil the bike, that's not a bad price.

So I think it's good to utilize the local bike shop. They know what they're doing. Just go in there and let them know you're willing to pay them for their services and that you want a good job. Don't try to cut down the price or you won't get as good a job. Tell them you want it done right and if they're a good racing shop they won't rip you off.

You certainly might want to hire a specialist to do the wheels. Most riders, after they've been in the sport for a year or so, learn to true up their own wheels. They learn the basics but they may not learn to build wheels or they may not want to.

Wheels are a common problem; they have to be kept in true. Every time you hit a pothole in the road it throws the wheel out a

maintenance and health

Wheels can go out of true from the stresses of riding. You can learn to do a certain amount of wheel trueing yourself but major wheel work is often a job for an expert.

little bit. Riding wheels that are not true is not a nice feeling and it wastes energy also, not having a round surface to ride on.

If you have any real wheel problems—if you're breaking a lot of spokes, for example—the best thing to do is have the wheel rebuilt. Take it to a reputable wheel builder or another rider who knows all about it, even if he charges you a fee to do it. Breaking spokes often happens when the hubs are not countersunk properly. There should be a 45-degree countersink where the spoke comes out of the hub, so that there's not a sharp angle pressing on the spoke.

HEALTH

Your body is a more important piece of equipment than your bicycle, so you should take care of it, too. This means eating the proper foods for health and fitness, taking care of any injuries or sicknesses that may occur, and being attentive to your own physical and mental well-being.

169

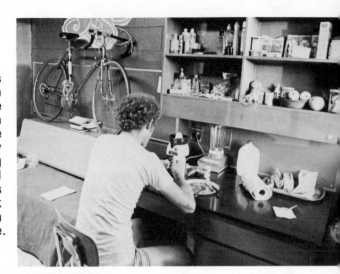

Although he was living away from home during the events, John Howard took care to eat properly before and during the National Championships and was at peak form when he won the road race.

What to Eat

If you are riding and racing regularly, you must take in a steady diet of all the elements that your body needs to perform well. This means protein, carbohydrates, fats, and vitamins. Because you have to perform every day, you must take in some of each of these every day. The simplest and best way to do this is to eat a balanced diet.

Complete protein comes from meat, fish, some dairy products, and certain combinations of vegetables. Carbohydrate comes from bread, potatoes, rice, and so-called starchy foods. Fats include both animal fats and vegetable oils. Vitamins are found in fresh fruit and green and yellow vegetables.

If you have something from each of these categories every day at almost every meal, you're really ahead of the game. You won't have to worry about vitamin supplements and you won't have to worry about any particular diet.

There are some special diets used by athletes, but they have their drawbacks. One is carbohydrate loading, where the athlete eats a lot of protein during the beginning of the week and then loads up on carbohydrates at the end of the week. That's great if

170

you're competing only on the weekend and your training is just for the day of competition. But if you're racing hard every couple of days or riding in a stage race, you must gear your diet to a more regular steady balanced intake.

Vegetarianism is OK, too. It is possible to get all the essential amino acids that make up good protein (usually found in meat) on a diet of grains, beans, and other vegetables. These things have to be eaten in the proper combinations, however, and can be time-consuming and expensive to buy and prepare. Sometimes you have to eat greater quantities, too, which can mess up your stomach.

I don't recommend taking vitamin supplements unless your diet is insufficient or erratic. Tablets take energy to digest and the system has to work longer and harder. If you keep putting all this stuff into your stomach, after a few days of racing you may have trouble digesting regular food. With a good healthful diet, you shouldn't need any supplements.

In any endurance event even a few extra pounds can hurt your performance, so weight is important. When you have more fat on your body, then you have more capillaries. It takes more effort for your heart to pump blood through these capillaries and the fat adds extra weight and slows down your cooling system.

During the off-season when you are not training as much, and particularly if you live in a cold climate, there is a tendency to put on weight. In order to keep warm in the winter, you start to crave things that are going to put a little more insulation (fat) on your body. That's one of the toughest things about living in a cold-weather climate; you start wanting sweets and cake and so on. You have to fight these cravings and try to stick to your regular diet. Your weight will go up anyway, from not riding as much.

This extra weight must be lost in the spring. If you lose it too quickly you won't ride as well, so try to go down slowly. Don't get so that you're not taking in enough food for the energy that you need. But the more fat you can get off yourself the better; there will still be plenty there.

A certain amount of weight is lost when you increase your training program, riding longer miles, but you must also cut down on carbohydrates and fats. This is very hard because if you don't have much carbohydrate your energy level goes down so you don't feel strong. You have to continue to eat enough for the training you're doing, keeping up energy but not eating an excess.

I really cut down on what I eat in the early season. I cut out fat almost completely by not eating any kinds of spreads or mayonnaise or fried foods (which are also hard to digest). There are enough fats in other foods to provide the necessities.

I do eat some carbohydrate to keep my energy level up. Usually my training is over in the morning; so at lunchtime, when I'm trying to lose weight, I don't have any carbohydrates at all. At supper I'll have a nice regular balanced meal.

Illness and Injuries

I wouldn't recommend riding with a fever, but with a cold I think it's perfectly all right to continue to train as long as you take precautions. Don't overextend yourself, because you do have to rest when you have a cold.

Because it takes strength and energy to digest food, it's good to cut down on eating when you have a cold. Eat light foods, first of all, because you won't be doing as much training. You want your strength to come back and you don't want to lose strength by having to digest food that's not going to be utilized anyway. Second, drink a lot of liquids. If you do have a fever, that will help keep your temperature down and, for some reason, it also seems to help flush out the cold.

By cutting down on food, drinking liquids, and getting a lot of rest, I have learned to get rid of a cold in a couple of days.

Boils and saddle sores are sometimes a problem for cyclists. They seem to come from ingrown hairs. Some little infection may start, which the pressure of the saddle aggravates. As you keep on riding it spreads from the inside and other ones come out, which are really painful.

The quickest way to get rid of boils and saddle sores is to stop riding. Every day you can put medicated soap in a hot bath, soak in it for a while, and then clean off with alcohol. For most people this will get rid of the sores in about three days. There are some iodine solutions, too, which are useful.

If you have to keep riding on a saddle sore it's rough going. Get some pain-deadening salve to put on it. I also put a lot of lubricant in the chamois of my tights. If worse comes to worse, you have to take aspirin, too. That's about all you can do about it.

Boils sometimes come from not having enough lubricant on the chamois. You must keep the chamois fairly clean, too. Wipe it off or wash it every time you use it. It helps to have a pair of tights for every day of the week at least. That's not a whole lot of tights, either; just for one six-day race I use 14 or 15 pairs.

Some people have trouble with the ligaments or cartilage in their knees in cold weather. This is probably from the way the muscles are pulling and the way the knee is bent, and trainers will always tell you to keep your knees warm in cold weather.

Varicose veins don't seem to affect anybody's riding. There's not much pain and little danger of blood clots because you're always active.

Cramps come mostly when you don't have enough miles in your legs. Sometimes they are caused by a lack of calcium or salt, but usually it's just a lack of training. The rest of your body might feel strong but your legs start to flutter and you can't do anything about it. All of a sudden your leg will feel like it's expanding, and then it will lock up.

If you feel a cramp coming on sometimes you can shake it by taking your foot out of the toe-clip and pedaling with your heel or instep. But the chances are that once it's started fluttering you're going to get it if you keep on pushing hard.

Massage—both before and after an event—is psychologically relaxing, which in turn makes it physically relaxing. It's nice to lay on that massage table; it's just like meditating. It takes your mind off everything and you feel just super. Real bike masseurs know how to rub and they talk to you when they're rubbing. The

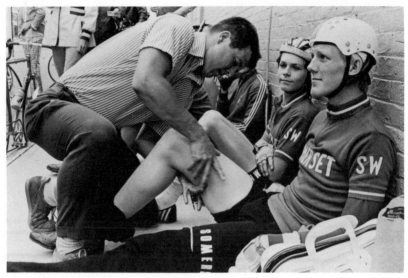
Massage is relaxing before or after an event.

bike rider has very soft supple muscles; the masseur slaps them around but in such a way that it feels like the muscles are hanging off the legs, nice and loose. When you get up from a good massage you feel really relaxed and refreshed.

Can You Train Too Much?

A person can get run down from not eating good food or not getting enough rest or sleep and so forth. You might get anemic, with a low blood count, and would have to eat foods that are going to help build up your red blood cells. Don't train hard until your blood count starts coming back up, because training in a weakened state is too frustrating; you tire quickly and get discouraged. Just go through the motions by doing a little riding, and visit a doctor. When your blood count improves, then you can increase your training and do a little more.

I don't think you can really hurt yourself by training, except that if you take a hundred-mile ride every day you might get a

Four times National Road
Champion, John Howard
trains hard all year long.

little bit tired. Or you might go out riding with someone who is
fitter than you are and blow yourself apart for a couple of days.
Then you would have to start building yourself up again by
maybe taking a day off or a few real easy days. Get back into
your regular schedule a few days later, when everything's back to
normal.

If you go out and do something you're not ready for, you will
feel the effects for several days. For example, if you take a tremendously long ride that you haven't built up to—say you've
been doing 25 miles and you try 100—on that ride you might feel
very light and very nice, especially in the first part of it. But if
the miles just aren't in your legs, you can wind up with cramps—
your legs just won't turn over. Your muscles are not conditioned
to perform for that long.

I don't think you can train too much if you build up to it.
Nobody trains as hard or as long as they're going to race, as they
would in a six-day or a stage race or whatever. You can ride
hundreds of miles day after day after day if you're prepared for it.

175

Bicycle racing is one of the most popular sports in the world, especially in Europe and Latin America. The U.S., however, was once the center of competition, and there are signs that cycling is experiencing a renaissance in this country. Thanks to increased fuel consciousness and national interest in health and fitness, bicycle racing should soon be as popular in the United States as it is overseas.

appendix I

how bicycle
racing is organized

Like most sports, bicycle racing is organized on local, state, regional, national, and international levels. The purpose of these organizations is to promote and supervise the sport, protect and regulate riders, make rules, train officials, select teams, and so on.

The first bicycle organization you meet may well be a local bicycle club. Club activities may include social and informational meetings, training rides, coaching, weekly race series, or promoting major events. Many clubs have commercial sponsors whose money helps support these activities; in return, the sponsor's name is printed on the club jersey.

It is the hundreds of racing clubs all over the country that form the organization known as the United States Cycling Federation. In return for its yearly membership fee, the club votes on legislation, as well as other matters, and elects the Board of Directors, which administers the day-to-day operations of the U.S.C.F.

To supervise clubs, races, and riders in each state, the U.S.C.F. appoints District Representatives. These officials also conduct the District Championships each year. On the regional level are other organizations of clubs or riders, such as the Northern California Cycling Association or the Southeastern Cycling Federation.

Besides appointing District Representatives, the U.S.C.F. sanctions races, selects international and Olympic teams, conducts the National Championships, maintains records, and licenses riders.

In order to compete in sanctioned races or be selected to important teams, an amateur rider must have a U.S.C.F. racing license. This is issued yearly; with it comes a rulebook and a subscription to the publication *Velo-news*, which contains a calendar of races, results, and other information necessary for competitors. Licensed riders agree to follow U.S.C.F. rules and may not compete against unlicensed riders except at the club level.

Riders compete according to age and sex. Classes include midget girls and midget boys (ages 8-11), intermediate girls and intermediate boys (ages 12 to 14), junior women and junior men (ages 15 to 17), senior women and senior men (ages 18 and older), and veteran men (age 40 and older). There are also Categories (I through IV), which divide riders by ability; these apply to senior men and some women and juniors. New license holders begin in Category IV and advance to a higher category by winning or placing in a certain number of designated races.

There are many big annual races or race series, but the most important are the District and National Championships. Any license holder is eligible to compete in his District Championships; top placers qualify for the Nationals. The District and National Championships consist of the following events:

Road: Veterans, senior men, senior women, junior men, junior women, intermediate boys, intermediate girls, and midget boys.

25-mile time trial: Veterans, senior men, senior women, and junior men.

Track, Senior men: Kilometer time trial, sprint, individual 4,000-meter pursuit, team pursuit, and ten-mile scratch.

Track, Senior women: Sprint and 3,000-meter individual pursuit. □

Track (other classes—one title is awarded in each class according to points earned in several races): Junior men, junior women, intermediate boys, intermediate girls, midget boys, and midget girls.

Cyclocross: Senior men, senior women, and juniors.

License forms and other information on racing are available from the U.S.C.F. office, Box 669, Wall Street Station, New York, NY 10005.

Professional riders in the United States are governed by the Professional Racing Organization of America (P.R.O.).

The international governing body of cycling is called the Union Cycliste Internationale (U.C.I.) and it has two branches. The professional branch is called the Fédération International de Cyclisme Professional (F.I.C.P.) and the amateur branch is the Fédération International Amateur de Cyclisme (F.I.A.C.). National governing bodies are responsible to these branches and to the U.C.I. The U.C.I. holds regular meetings, publishes the international calendar, licenses international officials, conducts the World Championships, and supervises cycling events at the Pan American and Olympic Games.

World Road, Track, and Cyclocross Championships are held every year for women (no cyclocross), juniors, amateur men, and professionals, except that the amateur men do not have Road and Track Championships during an Olympic year. The Olympics occur every four years (for amateur senior men only) and include a road race, a team time trial, kilometer, sprint, individual, and team pursuit. The Pan Am Games are held the year before the Olympics and include the same events.

appendix II

an explanation
of gearing

Each so-called "gear" on your bicycle is achieved by a combination of a certain front chain ring with a specific rear sprocket. The gear is described by the number of teeth in this combination and the front number is usually named first. Thus a 52-tooth front chain ring combined with a 14-tooth rear sprocket is called a "fifty-two fourteen." This is written 52 x 14.

Internationally, gears are also referred to by the distance the bicycle will travel with one revolution of the cranks. One revolution with a 52 x 14 will take you about 26 feet forward along the road. This is called "development."

In the United States, however, a more old-fashioned method is in common use, which compares the gear to the wheel diameter of a direct front-wheel-drive high-wheeler bicycle. The numbers are achieved by dividing the number of front teeth by the number of rear teeth and multiplying by the number of inches in diameter of the wheel (27 inches) for most adult racing bicycles.) The resulting number is proportionate to the international system and so is still a useful guide to gear relationships.

It is not important for you to be able to explain or compute these gears, but you should be familiar with the appropriate inches of your gear combinations. For example, a 52 x 14 in the American system is 100.3 inches.

The chart will also help you to see how your gears overlap. Notice that a 42 x 16 combination (70.9 inches) is almost equivalent to (but slightly larger than) a 52 x 20 (70.2 inches).

Number of teeth on rear sprocket

Number of teeth on front chain ring

	13	14	15	16	17	18	19	20	21	22	23	24	25	26	28	30	31
32	66.5	61.7	57.6	54.0	50.8	48.0	45.5	43.2	41.1	39.3	37.6	36.0	34.6	33.2	30.9	28.8	27.9
33	68.5	63.6	59.4	55.7	52.4	49.5	46.9	44.5	42.4	40.5	38.7	37.1	35.6	34.3	31.8	29.7	28.7
34	70.6	65.6	61.2	57.4	54.0	51.0	48.3	45.9	43.7	41.7	39.9	38.3	36.7	35.3	32.8	30.6	29.6
35	72.7	67.5	63.0	59.1	55.6	52.5	49.7	47.3	45.0	43.0	41.1	39.4	37.8	36.3	33.8	31.5	30.5
36	74.8	69.4	64.8	60.8	57.2	54.0	51.2	48.6	46.3	44.2	42.3	40.5	38.9	37.4	34.7	32.4	31.4
37	76.8	71.4	66.6	62.4	58.8	55.5	52.6	49.9	47.6	45.4	43.4	41.6	40.0	38.4	35.7	33.3	32.2
38	78.9	73.3	68.4	64.1	60.4	57.0	54.0	51.3	48.9	46.6	44.6	42.8	41.0	39.5	36.6	34.2	33.1
39	81.0	75.2	70.2	65.8	61.9	58.5	55.4	52.6	50.1	47.9	45.8	43.9	42.1	40.5	37.6	35.1	34.9
40	83.1	77.1	72.0	67.5	63.5	60.0	56.8	54.0	51.4	49.1	47.0	45.0	43.2	41.5	38.6	36.0	34.3
41	85.2	79.1	73.8	69.2	65.1	61.5	58.3	55.3	52.7	50.3	48.1	46.1	44.3	42.6	39.5	36.9	35.7
42	87.2	81.0	75.6	70.9	66.7	63.0	59.7	56.7	54.0	51.5	49.3	47.3	45.4	43.6	40.5	37.8	36.5
43	89.3	82.9	77.4	72.6	68.3	64.5	61.1	58.0	55.3	52.8	50.5	48.4	46.4	44.7	41.5	38.7	37.5
44	91.4	84.9	79.2	74.3	69.9	66.0	62.5	59.4	56.6	54.0	51.7	49.5	47.5	45.7	42.4	39.6	38.3
45	93.5	86.8	81.0	75.9	71.5	67.5	63.9	60.8	57.9	55.2	52.8	50.6	48.6	46.7	43.4	40.5	39.2
46	95.5	88.7	82.8	77.6	73.1	69.0	65.4	62.1	59.1	56.5	54.0	51.8	49.7	47.8	44.4	41.4	40.1
47	97.6	90.6	84.6	79.3	74.6	70.5	66.8	63.4	60.4	57.7	55.2	52.9	50.8	48.8	45.3	42.3	40.9
48	99.7	92.6	86.4	81.0	76.2	72.0	68.2	64.8	61.7	58.9	56.3	54.0	51.8	49.8	46.3	43.2	41.8
49	101.8	94.5	88.2	82.7	77.8	73.5	69.6	66.1	63.0	60.1	57.5	55.1	52.9	50.9	47.3	44.1	42.7
50	103.8	96.4	90.0	84.4	79.4	75.0	71.1	67.5	64.3	61.4	58.7	56.3	54.0	51.9	48.2	45.0	43.5
51	105.9	98.4	91.8	86.1	81.0	76.5	72.5	68.8	65.6	62.6	59.9	57.4	55.1	53.0	49.2	45.9	44.4
52	108.0	100.3	93.6	87.8	82.6	78.0	73.9	70.2	66.9	63.8	61.0	58.5	56.2	54.0	50.1	46.8	45.3
53	110.1	102.2	95.4	89.4	84.2	79.5	75.3	71.5	68.1	65.0	62.2	59.6	57.2	55.0	51.1	47.7	46.2
54	112.2	104.1	97.2	91.1	85.8	81.0	76.7	72.9	69.4	66.3	63.4	60.8	58.3	56.1	52.1	48.6	47.0

glossary

Ankling: Changing the angle of the foot when pedaling.

Apron: The optional flat area, specially surfaced, on the infield just inside and below the banked or racing part of a track.

Atmospheres: A measure of air pressure in the tires, which is described as a multiple of that at sea level.

Attack: To go at a faster pace in order to get away from another rider or group of riders.

Australian pursuit: An event on the track in which three or more riders start evenly spaced around the track and at the same time. Riders who are caught are removed from the race, which continues until there is only one man left.

Balancing: Maintaining the bike motionless on the track with the feet still in the pedals, a technique used by sprinters.

Banking: The main surface of a track, or more particularly the steepest area.

Blocking: To get in the way of other riders, as a tactic.

Blow up: To overexert oneself, run out of energy, or give up.

"Bonk, the": A feeling of complete physical collapse that comes when the rider runs out of energy.

Bottom bracket: The tube at the bottom of the frame that holds the crank assembly.

Break or breakaway: A group of riders that leaves the main group behind.

Bridge (a gap): To cross the space between one group of riders and another.

Bunch: See Field.

Chasers: Small groups or single riders trying to catch other groups.

Chucker: See Jamming tool.

183

Clinchers: A conventional bicycle tire with tube, which resembles an automobile tire in the way it is mounted on the rim.

Cluster: A group of gears fastened together and mounted on the rear wheel. Also called a block.

Cone nuts: Thin nuts that are screwed on the axle shaft to adjust and lock the wheel bearings.

Crank: The arm extending from the spindle of the bottom bracket assembly, upon which the pedals are mounted, or more properly the entire assembly (which includes those arms).

Criterium: A multilap road race on a short, usually closed, course.

Cross-three or cross-four: Refers to the pattern of spokes and how many other spokes each one crosses in its path from the hub to the rim.

Cups: Placed in the top and bottom of the head tube to hold the bearings in position.

Cyclocross: A bicycle event in which part of the course contains obstacles or difficult sections that must or may be covered on foot, carrying the bike.

Derailleur: A mechanical device used to shift the chain from one gear to another.

Drafting: Being protected from the wind by riding close behind another rider. Also called sitting in or pacing.

Echelon: A staggered line of riders, each one downwind of the one ahead.

Field: The main group of riders, also known as the pack or the bunch.

Field sprint: The finish among the main group of riders.

Fixed gear: A direct-drive chain and cog setup in which the rider cannot coast or shift gears.

Force the pace: To ride harder or attack.

Freewheel: The element in the rear gear setup that enables the rider to coast when not pedaling.

Half-wheeling: Staying a few inches ahead of another rider while riding alongside him in training.

Hammering: Riding hard.

Handicap: On the road, an event in which groups of riders start at different times, giving the slower ones an earlier start, etc. On the track, this is usually done by starting the riders on different lines instead of at different times.

Handsling: A method of changing partners in a team race.

Hang in: Barely keeping contact at the back of a group of riders.

Headset bearings: The small bearings located at the top and bottom of the head tube, which allow the fork to be held in position and move freely.

Hook: To move your back wheel as a threat, or by mistake, against the front wheel of another.

Interval training: A method, used in many sports, of short periods of near maximum effort interspaced with rest periods of minimum effort.

Italian pursuit: A form of team pursuiting on the track, with two teams of four or more men starting on opposite sides; each man drops out after he pulls a lap. The race ends with single riders on each team and the winning team is the one whose rider crosses his teams's line first.

Jamming: Riding hard.

Jamming tool: Also called a chucker. In team racing, an object that fits in the left hip pocket and is grasped by the partner to throw or relay the rider into the race.

Jump: To get out of the saddle and accelerate.

Kilometer: 1,000 meters, or the time trial event for one rider that covers this distance on the track.

Lay-back: The amount by which the seat is positioned behind the center of the cranks, or the angle of the seat tube that controls this.

Lead-out: A tactic or training activity in which one rider sprints for the benefit of the one behind him, who then comes by at an even greater speed.

Limit rider(s): In a handicap event, the rider or riders who have the shortest distance to travel.

Madison: A team race on the track in which riders on the same team relay each other into the race and take turns being in contention.

Mass start: Any event on the track or the road in which everyone starts at the same time and place. A scratch race.

Match sprint: A track event of two to four riders over the number of laps closest to 1,000 meters. The winner is the rider who crosses the line first. Time is taken on the last 200 meters.

Minute man or rider: In a time trial, the rider who starts one minute ahead of you is called your minute man.

Miss-and-out: Also called Devil-take-the-hindmost. A track event in which the last rider over the line on each lap or given number of laps is removed from the race.

Motorpace: To follow behind a vehicle with an engine; particularly, the event on the track involving pairs of motorcycles and bicycles.

Out-and-back: A course that goes to a certain point, makes a 180-degree turn, and comes back the same way. Usually used in time trials.

Pace line: A string of riders who alternately ride at the front and sit in.

Pack: See Field.

Pedal action: The turn of speed on the pedals.

Pick-up: Changing partners in a team race.

Point race: An event, on the track or the road, in which riders earn points by their placings in several finishes or primes throughout the race. The winner is not the first man to finish the race, but the one with the most points after the finish.

Point-to-point: A road race that is run from one place to another and that covers the course only once.

186

Pole line: The innermost line on the track, around which it is measured.

Pole, the: The area on a track between the pole line and the sprinters' line.

Prime: A sprint for points or prizes within a race. Not the finish.

Pull or pull through: To take a turn going hard at the front of a pace line or the field.

Pull off: To move to the side in order to let another rider come to the front.

Pursuit: A track event in which riders start on opposite sides and try to catch each other.

Road bike: A bicycle used for road racing and training on the road and that has several gears and at least one handbrake.

Road race: A general term for all events on the road, including time trials, criteriums, stage races, etc., but usually referring to a race of 25-100 miles over a large course.

Roller racing: Events, usually indoors, in which two or more sets of rollers are attached to some kind of distance recorder for the purposes of competition.

Rollers: An apparatus consisting of three cylinders joined by a drive belt and fitting the wheelbase of a bicycle, on which the cyclist can ride in place. Used for home training or exercise, for racing, and to warm up before events, especially at the track.

Runner: A dished section of the track between the banking and the apron or infield.

Scratch: The full distance in a handicap race, or an event in which everyone goes the same distance.

Scratch man or rider: The rider or riders in a handicap race who go the full distance and start "on scratch."

Scratch race: As opposed to a handicap race, an event in which everyone goes the full distance and starts at the same time and place.

Sew-up or tubular (tire): A tire in which the tube is sewn into the tire casing. It is attached to the rim with adhesive.

Sitting in: Drafting, or staying close behind another rider to be protected from the wind.

Six-day: An indoor track race, similar to a stage race on the road, which takes place over six days and is contested by teams of two or three riders, mostly in madison-style racing. The winner is the team that covers the greatest distance and/or wins the most points.

Sleigh riding: Sitting in, without doing any work at the front. Also called wheel-sucking.

Slipstream: The area of least wind resistance right behind another rider.

Snap: Quick acceleration ability.

Spindle: A central shaft in the bottom bracket assembly upon which bearings are mounted and to which the crank arms are attached. Can also refer to the axle in the hubs.

Sprint: A high-speed finish to a race or for a prime. Also, in track racing, the match sprint event.

Sprinters' line: A line 70 centimeters to the outside of, and running parallel to, the pole line. In the final 200 meters of some races, once the lead rider goes to the inside of the sprinters' line he is considered to have entered the pole and must stay inside of that line for the remainder of the race.

Stage race: An event consisting of several races—road, criterium, and time trial—which takes place over one day or more and in which the winner is the rider or team with the shortest total time for the combination of events.

Stayer bike: A bicycle used in the motorpace event, with a small front wheel, special fork, and other unique features.

Stayers' line: A line circling the track about halfway up, used in the motorpace event and in team racing.

String: In a race, a line of riders going off the front of the field or attacking.

Take a flyer: To ride off the front by yourself suddenly.

Tandem sprint: A track event for two riders on one bicycle (called a tandem). It is run like a match sprint, over the number of laps closest to 1,500 meters.

Team pursuit: A track event in which two teams of four start on opposite sides of the track and cover 4,000 meters to see which team finishes first. Time is taken on the third man.

Team race: Usually refers to the madison event on the track, a relay race.

Tempo riding: Training at a fast pace.

Time bonus: In a stage race, a number of seconds or minutes awarded to a rider or team for placing in a finish or prime, and which is subtracted from overall time.

Time trial: An event for individuals or teams that start separately and are timed over the distance. The winner is the one with the shortest time.

Toe in: A method of positioning the brake shoes whereby the front of the shoe strikes the rim first.

Track bike: A fixed-gear bicycle with no brakes or shifting mechanisms and that usually has steeper angles and a higher bottom bracket than a road bike.

Track race: Any event held on a bicycle track or velodrome.

Two-by-two method or formation: A training ride pattern commonly used in Europe, with pairs of riders making a double line.

Velodrome: A bicycle racing track, usually involving some buildings as well—grandstands, cabins, etc.—but not necessarily.

Wheel-sucking: In a race, drafting too much or refusing to take a turn at the front.

Wind up: To accelerate towards top speed.

index

index